TRUST ME, I'M

I'M

عربي

Trust me, I'm an Arab

Trust me, I'm an Arab

Unwritten Rules for Doing Business in the Arab World

Omar Bdour

Trust me, I'm an Arab

Unwritten Rules for Doing Business in the Arab World

First Edition
Copyright © 2020
by Omar Bdour
@omarrbdour

W: www.londonarabia.com
W: trustmeiamanarab.com
E: info@londonarabia.com
T: + 44 (0) 203 411 0876

Editor work,   Dr Amber Roy
Design work, George Chipuc
              & Tamara Dias

ISBN 978-1-8382911-0-5

Also available as an eBook

ISBN 978-1-8382911-1-2

Printed in the United Kingdom

Published by London Arabia

@londonarabia

Acknowledgements

This book began as a big, messy project which required several contributors to shape it. Indeed, writing a book is harder than I originally thought, but it has been more rewarding than I could have ever imagined.

How does a person say "thank you" when there are so many people to thank? This book is a thank you for all the people who supported me during my work and helped me to reach this point. None of this would have been possible without the help and support of my family and friends. First and foremost, thank you to my children Adam, Safaa and Radwa, for their love and support. I offer great thanks to Sir Hugh Robertson for his kind foreword, and to all my family and friends who read my early drafts and for those who kindly gave me their advice on the name and cover design. I am also thankful to all the individuals I have had the opportunity to lead, be led by, or watch their leadership from afar.

And finally, I am forever grateful to the people who, for whatever reasons, decided to read my book.

Contents

Inside the book, I will try to help you to understand the Arab world in just a few words and through a small graphics sum up in single images what some studies spend thousands of words trying to explain. I visualises the cultural differences between the West and the Arab world in contrasting pairs of pictograms. With yellow symbolising the Arab world and blue representing the West.

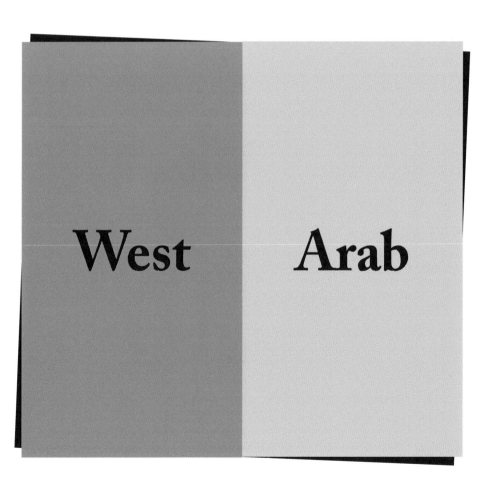

About the Author

Omar Bdour is the CEO of London Arabia Organisation. He is also the CEO of the Arab Women of the Year Awards, which was founded in 2014 in conjunction with Regents University London and the Bicester Village Shopping Collection and supported by the Mayor of London Office. The objectives of the organisation are to strengthen the cultural and business ties between the UK and the Arab world.

Omar oversees three projects that aim to do just that. The Arab Women of the Year Awards highlights the amazing achievements made by Arab women, London Arabia Art & Fashion Week which celebrates incredible Arab culture in London, and the London Arabia Magazine which provides another way of encouraging Arabs in the UK to integrate with British societies. London Arabia also provides tailored cultural training programs, which cater to companies working or selling to the Arabs in the west or doing business with the Arab world.

Omar's ambition is to increase cultural and business links between Britain and the Arab world. In today's increasingly globalised and intercultural world it is vitally important to understand other cultures in business. The large differences between British and Arab cultures can become a negative factor when businesses and people work together. Omar strives to show this does not have to be the case.

Each of the initiatives of the organisation helps Omar to promote cultural ties between Britain and the Arab world. They help to promote bilateral cultural, trade and investment between the United Kingdom and the Arab world. To achieve this Omar worked in close co-operation with Arabs and British government officials, Arab and British Universities, businesses, luxury brands and Arab diplomatic missions in London and British diplomatic missions in the Arab world. Omar trains and advises businesses, diplomats, and officials by helping them raise their cultural intelligence and encouraging a greater understanding between Britain and the Arab world. He has moderated and spoken at different events on the subject of Arab women and cross-cultural communications.

He has a background in public relations, communications, and media, and has worked to integrate the UK and the Arab world. He holds a BA in political science and, before his current post, he worked for the Arab British Chamber of Commerce from 2007-15 as Director of Public Relations and Events. He also helped establish LocalArabia, the first bilingual Arabic- English newspaper in London in 2005.

You might ask yourself, can an Arab person write about his culture and be fair, honest and unbiased? As an Arab living in the West, Omar is aware that some of the generalisations of Arabs and Westerners may be regarded as exaggerations. However, Omar's aim to express the typical stereotypes to attempt to break them down and allow relationships between Western and Arab people to blossom.

Foreword

Like many in the West, I have had a lifetime's fascination with the Arab world. I was a soldier there during the first Gulf War and, more recently, The Minister of State responsible for the Middle East and North Africa in The Foreign and Commonwealth Office. I have travelled across the region extensively and tried to do business there - with differing degrees of success. For a westerner new to the region and its people, it can be a confusing and, at times, a forbidding place. Yet, once you get to know it, the warmth of its landscapes and its people quickly impress.

I was delighted to hear that Omar Bdour had written this book with the specific aim of helping western businesses understand and navigate the region and its peoples. Omar has the advantage of straddling both cultures and of having spent fifteen years trying to help the West and the Arab world work better together. It is a timely and useful book, particularly in a period when the UK is looking to recalibrate its relationships beyond its European neighbours and at a time when the Arab world is frequently misrepresented and misunderstood in the West.

The Middle East and the Arab world are slightly different entities, but both contain the earliest cradles of civilisation and house many ancient seats of learning. They have a history that is rich, extensive and, at times, brutal. Many different peoples and cultures have interacted with the region. Then, as now, it sits at the crossroads of the world, buffeted by internal and external forces, and is constantly evolving. Both economically and culturally, it will continue to exert an influence on our lives here in the West for many years to come.

I would, therefore, encourage everyone not only to read and follow Omar's advice but also to invest some time understanding the Arab world and getting to know its people. It is an investment that will be repaid many times over.

Rt Hon Sir Hugh Robertson KCMG
28 October 2020

Notes

• For readability reasons there is no parallel use of male and female expressions. All terms used throughout the book to denote persons refer to both gender.

• The repetition in this book is intentional and is intended for those who might read the book out of sequence.

• Cultural patterns are only guidelines; it doesn't mean that everyone you meet will behave in the same way. There are only tendencies and every person must be treated as an individual.

• The advice contained in this book may not be suitable for your situation and you should consult with a professional where appropriate.

• Some of the information in this book may already be familiar to many people, and if so, please be patient and temporarily put aside what you know and your individual experience.

"When reading this book, you might think that some of my comments are offensive to some people in the Arab world or in the West. You might accuse me of profiling, and you question how can I make generalisations about almost half a billion people in the Arab world. Also, my tone at times may seem critical of Arabs and the Westerners. This is not my intention. I have the utmost respect for both cultures, and the aim of this book is not to criticise Arabs or Westerners. In fact, I aim to try in my small way to find a way to bridge the gap between Westerners and Arabs."

Omar Bdour

PREFACE

Everyone is Unique

When I first arrived in Europe, I was so confused when I saw people use their car's headlights to allow others to pass or to give way. In the Arab world, a driver uses their headlight to tell the person wanting to cross the road that they are not giving way. I have used this example to demonstrate that even the simple things in life can be different and people can mean and interpret things differently. You might visit a new country and wonder about the way people in that country speak to each other, think, act, or even cross the road. The custom of a certain culture can play a key role in shaping the form of a country. A country's culture, religion, language, family and how they do business are important factors in how people act. You might believe that you will not be exposed to different examples of culture, but there will always be new behaviours that will be experienced when you go to a new place. These new behaviours also explain why you might experience culture shock when you move to a new country or start interacting with a new group of people who have very different attitudes and beliefs from the ones you are used to.

For instance, you sit in your office on a rainy London day -or a sunny California day - spinning your silver globe and wondering where you should expand your business next and what to do after the 2020 Covid-19 crisis. Your thoughts automatically slide towards the Arab world, perhaps due to the location of that part of the world, nestling between Europe, Asia, and Africa. Many Western business and businesspeople are now thinking of moving East. Many of them believe that business in the Arab world is one of the safest exit strategies from this crisis.

Business activities with the Arab World are very rewarding. Millions of Westerns businesses have already established connections with the Arab world. Daily, these connections are expanding, this is why awareness of Arab cultural similarities and differences is essential for a successful business. But how much do you know about the Arab world, culture, and people?.

My Generalisations

Trust me, I'm an Arab, stems from my interests into the history and culture of the Arab world as well as the cultural shock I have witnessed when working in both Western and Arabic contexts. The aim of this book is to enhance the success of Western business, institutions, or individuals, private or public sectors when dealing with Arab people.

I will be making some generalisations about the Arab world. I make these generalisations as an Arab person who has worked, seen and experienced both Western and Arab cultures. All the information has been collated from many years of working in the West and dealing with the Arabs who want to visit the UK for business or pleasure and with Westerners who want to visit the Arab world and do business there.

My views and generalisations, of course, do not cover all individual differences. It is important to understand that many sections within this book are generalisations and will not cover every situation you might face. For example, I can generalise that Arab people always arrive late, or some Arab women may not shake hands with men. Yes, this does occur, and you might face this during your time in the Arab world, but you might also experience the opposite.

Anyone thinking of doing business with the Arabs, and those who are visiting, or have any kind of interests in the region will benefit from this book. It will also be of use to also people who deal with the Arabs in the West from the luxury industries, tourism, business executives at all levels, diplomats, government officials and students.

However, it is important to remember that there will always be exceptions to any rule! Everyone, no matter what their cultural background, has different opinions, habits, and ways of life. The sooner that you accept that everyone is different, the easier it will become to understand and embrace cultural differences. It is important to realise the certain Arab behaviours that appear in this book do not apply to all Arabs; it does not mean all Arabs act, think, and believe the same thing.

It is almost impossible to account for the diversity within the Arab world. So, when trying to understand the Arab culture, you must treat people and situations individually. Some individuals may not care about their own cultural rules, for instance. It is the hope that this book will aid your ability to spot different behaviours which are part of and differ from, the Arab way of life.

TRUST ME,
I'M

عربي

1 Introduction

Stereotypes of the Arab World

When I advise Westerners about Arab culture, especially if they have never been to the Arab world, I stress that they should not be fooled by what they hear about the region and that they should remember to apply the same basic business principles in the Arab world that they use successfully in the West. One of the biggest difficulties to overcome in understanding cultural differences is making judgements based on one opinion. People sometimes ask me questions, such as 'can I argue with an Arab?', 'Is it true that Arab women must walk a few metres behind their husbands?. That is why, as a Westerner, it is very important that you do your own research and make an effort to actually learn about the history, religion, language, and culture of the Arab world.

When Westerners first hear the word 'Arab', the primary thing that often comes to their minds is the tired stereotype of that region, a stereotype which has a long history. If you read the nineteenth-century orientalist writers' works about their travels to the Arab world, you will only see descriptions of poverty, a backward way of life, savages, and lawless Arabs. At the time, the Westerners who had never visited the region based their interpretations of the Arab world on these writers and sometimes also from the translations of the "Arabian Nights", which contained images of a desert region, run by nomads with camels, a seated prince surrounded by dancing women, and a lot of blood, violence and death. Unfortunately, these comments and descriptions still have political implications to this day.

In the 20th century, the rhetoric surrounding the Arab world tended to be all about oil, wealth, and religious conflicts. In recent years, it has been about war and terrorism, political unrest, and religious problems. To some, Arabs are seen as people who lack intelligence, people who live in a region that has not learnt to live in peace. In London, the Arab world is associated with women in the veil, sports cars owned by the oil-rich and luxury shoppers in West London. In daily Western culture, Arabs are often stereotyped this way or very similarly.

These stereotypical assumptions tend to ignore the majority of the Arabs. This causes the feeling that Westerners are uninformed about the Arab world. Unfortunately, many Westerners welcome and agree with these stereotypes. No one can deny the fact that there are few reports which balance the information about ordinary people with normal lives, who live and work in Arab regions. One of the worst stereotypes can be seen every time an incident such as an attack or bombing occurs. Westerners often hole unsubstantiated suspicion and criticism of Arab and Muslim people living in the West. For the majority of these people, the minute there is news of an incident, the first thing they do is pray that it is not a terrorist attack and that it does not involve a Muslim. Due to the stereotypical suspicion and criticism, Arab people living in the West often do not want anything to do with even an attack on them, simply because they are tired of the negative news about them.

Western Disney Characters   **Arab Disney Characters**

In the West, the majority of television programs show Arabs as terrorists, dictators, and wealthy playboys. In movies, the image of "false-hearted" Arabs is common. For instance, if we look at "The Sheik" movie of 1921 *(Aljazeera, 2020)* we can see such misconceived stereotypes. "The Sheik" was based on the Arabian night's literature, but a new element was added to the film that we cannot read in the books of the orientalist writers. The new scene which was added shows 'the blond innocent woman' whom the Arab men are obsessed with and attempt to win her in any way possible. This was repeated in almost every Hollywood movie about the Arabs thereafter. Another added element in Hollywood was the white male Knight, who was depicted as strong, handsome, noble, and intelligent. The white man was shown as superior to not only the Arabs but also to Black, Asians and American Indians. All women in the film adored him, while the evil Arab man was hated by all women; even the Arab women despised the Arab man and fell in love with the Knight. Even so, Arab women were not separated from stereotypes. Arab women always appear as dancers for the prince's "Hareem" and slaves to his desires.

Even in Disney World, which targets young children, Arabs are portrayed with negative images, women are belly dancers and men are violent terrorists and religious extremists. This is how the Western media, such as Hollywood and Disney, shape the public's perceptions of the Arab world and its people.

Many misconceptions and stereotypes still exist to this day. Many Westerners apply general stereotyping to the Arab world, no matter how open-minded they are. In the Arab world, particularly in business, many intellectual and well-educated people have built wealth through very smart business negotiations. Their intellect, knowledge and business success means that you will create an easy business deal with them if you put aside all stereotypes and do not underestimate what they have and what they can offer. As a business, you must see beyond the stereotypes. In fact, once you learn about Arab culture and begin to build some interest, you will be surprised how fascinating and attractive it becomes.

No matter if you are visiting the GCC or the North African countries, you will see and hear things like, "is it dangerous for Westerners to be in that part of the world?", or "they do not like us" or "women should not go there, they will force her to cover up". Do not be put off by the misleading reports you see on social media and in the news.

The Business Practice

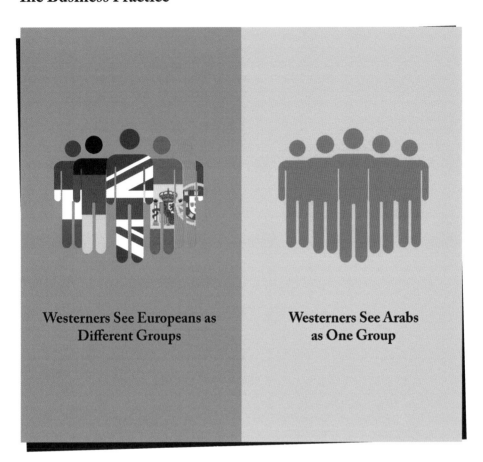

Westerners See Europeans as Different Groups

Westerners See Arabs as One Group

Let us do a small exercise!

Think about Europe. Do you see all Europeans as the same or different?

Now do the same for the Arab world. Do you think about people in the Arab world the same way that you think about Europeans?

It is rare for a Westerner to consider all Europeans as the same. Yet, Arab people are often seen as the same, despite the variety of states within the Arab world. If you say Italians and English are the same, then you can say Saudis and Egyptians are the same as well, but the truth is that Arabs are all different, just as all Europeans are. Arabs write and speak one language but with different dialogues and dialects, so they even find it difficult to understand each other.

Through my experiences visiting the Arab world, on my own, with colleagues and with business delegations and officials, I have witnessed cultural blunders by the Westerners in the delegations and the shock experienced by the Arabs over how the situations were handled. With the correct cultural knowledge, all such mistakes could have been avoided.

To succeed in doing business in the Arab world, you and everyone at your business must understand the ups and downs with the Arab market and the sensitivities of its culture to cope with the differences between the West and the Arab World.

While doing business with people from other nations, a sense of dealing with conflicting approaches is inevitable. Arabs have a strong value system, deeply influenced by Islam. The role of the family, personal dignity, social morality and respect for children and the elderly are all beliefs of this religion. Hospitality, generosity, and politeness are also highly valued and expected from the individual. Far more than in Western society, there is a keen sense of tradition and a belief that fate also plays a significant role in life. These values are often different from Western culture and lack of knowledge of them can offend. Many other misunderstandings between the Arabs and Western cultures exist around the way language is used, how an Arab person is addressed, at the topics of conversation.

The Book

This book is written for and dedicated to the many people and businesses thinking of, or already doing, business in the Arab world. Of course, there is no shortage of books advising Westerners on what they should do when they are in the Arab world, but this book differs by making it easier for you to put the advice into practice; this book is a current and up to date comparative guide of the differences between the Western and Arab worlds. It addresses the real, day to day problems that businesses face in the Arab world, for example, how to sign a contract and enforce it when you know that your Arab partner will not abide by it.

The information in this book focuses on the differences you will see and face as a Westerner in the Arab world or dealing with Arab people. It will walk you through the differences between the two cultures and what to do to reduce the chance of cultural blunders. The book will show you the value of understanding these differences as well as what is and is not acceptable to Arabs and what their expectations from you. You will learn how to make friends with Arab people and how to negotiate with them.

It is the aim that through explanation of background behaviours and rationale for Arab attitudes, which can be confusing to Westerns, this book will lead readers to understand the Arab culture. It is the hope of this book that will help people to create successful partnerships between the Western and Arab world.

Chapter one introduces the topic of the book and demonstrates the importance of the book. It introduces you to what you should expect when reading the book and how stereotypes of the Arab world might affect your business.

Chapter two explains what culture is, some of the basics of Arab culture and why it is important. This chapter also discusses if the Arab culture is one culture or several, what the differences between the Arabs are and why, as a westerner, you should not ignore the importance of culture even when you already have some experience with dealing with the Arabs. This will be followed by an introduction to the Arab World and its history in Chapter three. Which will also allow you to understand the term 'Middle East', the people living there, the importance of business in each geographic group, the Arab attitudes towards Westerners.

Chapter four sheds light on the new middle class in the Arab world. Chapter five focusses on the Arab contributions to civilisation, while Chapter six covers the important aspect of how religion and Islam can shape your relationships with your Arab counterpart. This chapter will introduce you to the importance of the five pillars of Islam and the Arab Christians.

Chapter seven will highlight the importance of family to the Arabs and its structure and impact on doing business. Chapter eight focuses on the Arabic language and how language differs across the Arab world. Chapter nine moves on to discuss Arab women, the misconception on the west and women's roles in the Arab world. Arab hospitality and its important for business is focused on in Chapter ten, this chapter teaches you how to behave when at home and how to dine with the Arabs. It also introduces you to how to be a perfect guest and how to dress. Chapter eleven explains Arab personalities and curiosity, how the compliment and the power of words, while Chapter twelve explains the use of social media in the Arab world.

Chapter thirteen considers how to do business, and how you should modify your behaviour when in the Arab world. This chapter covers the ways of initiating contact and meetings, how to arrive at your meetings, what to talk about and how to plan your agenda and follow up the meeting. It also explains what to include in your presentation and the use of English. This is followed by chapter fifteen which looks at the common Arab approaches and how the Arabs negotiate and the tactics they use in closing a deal. This chapter will also discuss how you should prepare yourself and the effect of honour, shame, hierarchy, and body language on a deal. Chapter sixteen briefly talks about the risks and opportunities involved in doing business in the Arab world, and the book culminates with chapter seventeen, the conclusion.

TRUST ME,
I'M

عربي

2

Culture

Is the Arab Culture One Culture or Several?

The Arab world is full of rich and diverse communities, ethnicities groups and cultures. So, there is not one clear set of etiquette rules. Differences exist not only among countries but also within countries. It is therefore important to be aware of the diverse ways people behave and live. For instance, Lebanon is a country with many Western attitudes, whereas there is a much stricter Muslim attitude in Saudi Arabia. Both differing attitudes are found in the United Arab Emirates where a very modern and western way of life can be found in Dubai, but the rules are much stricter half an hour away in Sharjah.

What is Culture?

There are many different ways to describe what culture is. The definition which I prefer what *(Samovar and Porter, 1994)*, articulate of culture: "The cumulative deposit of knowledge, experience, beliefs, values, attitudes, meanings, hierarchies, religion, notions of time, roles, spatial relations, concepts of the universe, and material objects and possessions acquired by a group of people in the course of generations through individual and group striving". While this is the definition of culture that I will focus on in the book, there is also another definition which refers to culture as being defined as an appreciation of the arts and human intellectual achievement. In both views of culture, examples are a good way to quickly understand culture.

Why does Culture Matter?

All of us have been taught and told how to behave and what is classed as good manners from a very young age by our parents and guardians. We learn other behaviours automatically through our dealing with others in our daily life, but those behaviours and manners apply to our own traditions, culture and country and often do not apply to other cultures and countries. If we are unaware of the differences when we are abroad then we may not notice that a social blunder has occurred. Such mistakes even happen to ex-pats. Without the proper knowledge, what you think is normal can cause offence and, as a result, you may lose a business contract without knowing the reason behind it.

Developing an understanding of other cultures and how to interact with people from different cultures is an integral component of a business and can greatly affect the sale of products. However, working and doing business abroad can be difficult and confusing. Other cultures do things differently: the people often behave and think differently; they look and dress differently, and the food they share is also often very different. It is then no surprise that other countries and cultures will also have other ways to carry out business. Many contracts and business opportunities have been lost because cultural rules have been ignored. A cultural blunder can be the start of the end for a business deal. Cultural blunders are usually caused by a poor understanding of the importance of cultural awareness.

The success or failure of any business or brand depends on individuals within those businesses and their knowledge of the impact of cross-cultural differences on business. Lack of knowledge and preparation increases the likelihood that misunderstandings will occur. Such misjudgement can result in expensive mistakes that could have been avoided.

Frequently, individuals who are newly exposed to a different culture are not prepared for the experience and will go through what is called a "culture shock." They may be confused when a normal statement offends, if a serious statement is not taken seriously, or if humour is misunderstood. Undoubtedly, the misinterpretation of normal business practice will result in frustration. Considering the way the global economy is moving it is especially important to invest in cultural awareness to avoid such mistakes. If your business is expanding abroad make cultural awareness a core part of the recruitment process for international business.

What is Arab Culture and why is it Important?

Handshake or a Hug?

Imagine that your company is about to launch a new line of luxury sweet and chocolate into the Saudi market. You have done all the work and everyone has assured you that a luxury product will sell well in Saudi as it has a big market for luxury products. You were not aware that alcohol and pork gelatine are forbidden in Saudi Arabia, because of their religious beliefs. Unfortunately, the sweet and chocolate contain alcohol and pork gelatine. All your preparations cannot go ahead and the opening of stock and shipments will cost your company a fortune. As a result, your boss is angry, and your job is in danger.

If business people can learn more about the culture and values of the Arab world, and why those customs and values are important for the Arabs, then businesses may find themselves more aware and have a greater understanding of the Arab values in business proceedings. It is very important to be aware of cultural and religious considerations when you do business in the Arab world. For Arabs, business is personal, so it can bring honour and hospitality into a business deal.

Business opportunities in the Arab world are expanding as is the awareness of its culture, how it is different and what should not be done during business. A huge number of Westerners do business outside of their countries and a lot of them see the Arab world is an important destination to expand. However, if the sensitive nature of this part of the world is not fully understood then an expansion in business will be difficult to start. Knowledge of basic things, such as how to shake hands, when to make eye contact, how to address people of different genders and what to say or not to say can considerably aid business expansion. For example, saying 'I don't know' is considered rude and is often interpreted as an inability or lack of knowledge in closing a deal.

In the Arab world, you will meet very smart people who have a greater understanding of western culture than some western has of theirs. Also, while respecting and learning about their culture is important, mistakes are mostly ignored as a cultural faux pas as long as they were not intentionally rude or disrespectful to their culture. It is not necessary or appropriate to be culturally judgmental when conducting business with Arab people.

How much do I need to Learn?

The simple answer, every situation is different. According to *(Bochner, 1982)*, "Intercultural contacts can be classified into two broad categories: those that occur among the residents of a culturally diverse nation or society and those that take place when a person from one society travels to another country with a particular objective in mind; for example, to work, play, study, exploit, convert, or provide assistance".

During Donald Trump's first campaign to become the US president, he insulted and demonized Arabs and Muslims all over the world. However, he changed his narrative once he became president. Trump chose a Muslim and Arab country to be the first country in the world to visit as US president in order to try to recover from his blunders and insults. He used the visit to talk about Islam and the Arab world in a completely different way in an attempt to change his image.

Culture is personal and changes depending upon the circumstances and the people you are dealing with. Arab Culture is also changing; many Arab countries have become much more modern, as many traditional attitudes and business practices evolve towards a more Westernised approach. But this does not mean that Arabs are also changing the way they live, even if they have been increasingly exposed to Western cultural values over the last decades. With increasing numbers of the younger generations of wealthy Arab families being educated in the West, international business practices are becoming more common, however, this does not mean that they are moving away from the principle of the culture itself.

When in Arabia, do as the Arabs do

When in the Arab world, do as the Arabs do. This means that you should understand and adapt to the Arab culture; it does not mean that you should try to become an Arab. Arabs like to understand who you are and what kind of a person they are dealing with. Therefore, it is important to understand them but also to be yourself and give them the time to understand you.

When dealing with Arabs it is sometimes very confusing, no matter which country or in which sector you are in; from a very senior executive in business meetings in an Arab country to a small shop or a hotel desk in the West. The stereotypes introduced previously may be in the mind of many of the Westerners when they deal with Arabs. This adds further confusion to the proceedings, and they may ask themselves or their colleagues, "why can't they say yes or no? Why doesn't he/she tell me if he/she doesn't understand something?"

You might be thinking 'why do I need to learn about the Arab culture?' and 'how do the Arabs behave?' Many businesses in the west believe that everyone outside the west is keen to learn the western way of doing business and western business etiquette. Therefore, some believe that non-Westerners must behave as the Westerners behave and do business in a western way. This is reasonable when you are in a western country, but it will cost you time and money when you expand into the Arab world.

I hear that you are thinking that Western companies have successfully carried out business in the Arab world for many decades without any problems. This is true, for decades' Western companies and people have been doing business in the Arab world, mainly in the Gulf Cooperation Council "GCC" countries, and have had very little competition.

Yet, it would be foolish to be misled into thinking that you can do business with the Arabs without understanding the ways in which they behave and do business. Besides the many social differences between Arabs and Westerns, today some of the world's largest economies, including China, Russia, India, Turkey, and Korea, have their presence and influence in the Arab world. It is thus evident that there are many different cultural ways to do business in the Arab world. Moreover, many Western organisations are feeling the impact that a lack of cultural sensitivity can inflict upon business performance.

Making assumptions can cause problems...

"We do not need it; We have been doing business there for 60 Years"

"The western way of working has worked for the Westerners in the Arab world for the past decades, and it will still work for them now"

"We have had a successful business in the Arab world for many years, why should I change a perfect business method?"

"As long as they speak English, everything will be OKAY"

TRUST ME,
I'M

عربي

3
The Arab World

The Middle East - East of What?

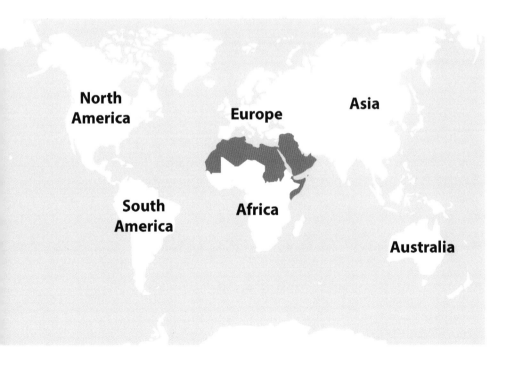

The easiest way to classify the Arab world is through the 22 member countries of The League of Arab States, or Arab League, a voluntary association of countries whose peoples are mainly Arabic speaking or where Arabic is an official language, which was founded in 1945 in Cairo *(BBC 2017)*. The idea of the Arab League was presented in 1942 by the British, who wanted to have the support of the Arab countries against the Alliance at that time. Despite the British intervention, the League was properly established just before the end of the Second World War.

The league once referred to all Arab countries, but this definition can be inaccurate as the organization includes countries that are not distinctive Arab countries, such as Somalia and Djibouti. Members of the league include Algeria, Bahrain, Comoro Islands, Djibouti, Egypt, Iraq, Jordan, Kuwait, Lebanon, Libya, Mauritania, Morocco, Oman, Palestine, Qatar, Saudi Arabia, Somalia, Sudan, Syria, Tunisia, United Arab Emirates, and Yemen.

It is also important to note that the Arab league is seen across the Arab world as ineffective in its conflict resolution within and between Arab countries. It has no impact nor respect amongst the Arab public.

History

To explain the Arab world, we have to talk about its history and how the past is important to the present time. This is a vast amount of information that, unfortunately, cannot all be covered here.

Arabs were only present in the Arabian Peninsula before the arrival of Islam. Many Arabs and Muslims can trace much of their heritage to the birth of the Prophet Muhammad in 570 A.D. The time before Islam is generally referred to as "the time of ignorance"*(Metz 1992)*. However, after 570 A.D, Prophet Muhammad's tribe had become active traders and established relationships with tribes all over the peninsula. These relationships allowed them to trade with Yemen and Syria and helped them to establish their new power and status among other tribes.

Prophet Muhammad controlled a large part of the surrounding regions and signed many treaties with non-Muslims. By his death in 632, his successors, who were called the "*Caliphs*", ruled the Islamic world and expanded its empire. In a short time, the Islamic world became a large empire set against the Roman and Persian empires. The "Caliphs" created one of the largest empires in history, it spread through the Arabian Peninsula, Levant and into North Africa and southern Spain. Non-Muslims (Christians and Jews) were also part of this Arab society. The Arab empire expanded very fast reaching Europe through Spain and established Arab control of areas between Spain to Pakistan.

During this period, the Arab empire was threatened by other empires, the Ottoman Turks (a Muslim empire) and the Mongols.

The Ottoman Empire ruled the Arab world until World War I, after which the Western powers, including Britain and France, ruled many parts of the Arab world. It was not until the early 1970's that many of the Arabs became completely independent.

The Arab world meets Asia and Africa and borders Europe, which makes it one of the world's most strategic regions. It stretches from the Atlantic coast of northern Africa in the West to the Arabian Sea in the east, and from the Mediterranean Sea in the north to Central Africa in the south. An expanse of more than 5 million square miles, almost double the size of the USA, at 3.6 million square miles. The majority of the Arab world territory is in Africa and with only around one quarter in Asia.

The Arab world is also known as the Middle East and North Africa (MENA). Although this excludes Somalia, Djibouti, and the Comoros Islands which are part of the Arab world. The Arab countries share one language, one history, and a very old culture. In 2020, the total population of the Arab world amounted to approximately "436 million people" *(United Nation, 2020)*.

The Oil Discovery

The discovery of oil in the region was a big turning point in the region's history. First oil discovered in an Arab nation was in 1908, As car ownership grew so did the demand for oil to make the gasoline used as fuel. At this time oil was also discovered in the Middle East *(BBC)*. By the 1970's, oil had afforded Western companies business opportunities and economic influence in the Arab world. As a result, foreign companies and powers began to focus great attention on the Arab market. In 1975, the opening of the Suez Canal allowed that part of the world the opportunity to play a big part in trade between West and East. This also occurred during the Arab-Israelis war, 1973, when mostly the GCC countries greatly increased the price of oil and therefore increased profits for the majority of the Arab oil countries. During this time, Saudi and Egypt were the most powerful Arabic countries. Saudi had the world's largest oil reserve and Egypt, benefitted from its large population and location in a strategic eastern Mediterranean location, ideal for trade and oil transit.

The Middle East

The term the Middle East is known and used all over the world, but you might hear some say there is no 'east' in the Middle East. If you are familiar with the world geography you will ask, if the Middle East includes North Africa and West Asia, then what is it the east and middle of who?

Many people all over the world do not understand the separation between the Arab world and the Middle East, even though there is a large distance between both areas. North African countries are also a long way from the Middle East, and both areas are very different. If you visit a north African country you will notice the difference in every aspect of life, from the way they live, their food and how they do business. However, the Middle East refers to and includes all of North Africa because they are Arab and Muslim.

The word "Middle East" is a political concept, created by the British India Office in the 1850's. At that time, the term Orient was the term used to describe the east to people in the West. The Orient was split into three parts, the Near East, the Middle East and the Far East, to describe the area between the British colony of India and the Near East (the Balkans and Western part of the Ottoman Empire). It is important to remember that this term was created from a Western geographical perspective; if the Indian or Chinese had the power during that time, they might have called this region the Middle West, not the Middle East.

Some have suggested that the term "Middle East" is problematic because it is, undeniably, a Western term reflecting a Western perspective. India's first prime minister, Jawaharlal Nehru, once observed that the region should really be called West Asia, and there have been occasional efforts to adopt terms like "Southwest Asia" in academic circles *(Danforth, N (2016)*. Today, the use of this suggested name can be seen with some small organisations, such as the West Asian football league which includes part of the Arab world and Asia.

Not all Arabs are Muslims

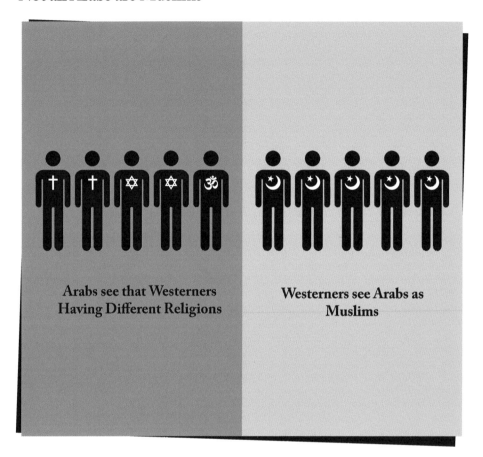

Arabs see that Westerners Having Different Religions

Westerners see Arabs as Muslims

While the majority of Arabs are Muslim, approximately 10% of Arabs are not. Arabs comprise just 12% of the world's Muslim population, Arab culture also includes Christians, Jews, and many other religious beliefs. Almost one-sixth of the world's population are Muslims, the largest is in Indonesia and the Indian subcontinent. Therefore, not all Arabs are Muslims, and not all Muslims are Arabs. Moreover, not all Arab persons live within Arab culture, many live in non-Arab countries like the UK or the USA, but they maintain their Arab culture as part of their identity.

You will find that non-Arab Muslims in the Middle Eastern countries like Iran and Turkey share many of the attitudes and religious beliefs with the Arabs. Yet, their languages are different, and they are not Arabs. There is not a good relationship between Iran and Turkey and different parts of the Arab world. This tension is often increased between Iran and parts of the Arab world due to the different sectors of Islam within Iran that are different to the majority of the Arab world. It is also important to remember that mistaking Iranians, Turks and Arabs or any other groups in the region as one another will not be appreciated.

Aren't all Arabs the Same? No, it is Complicated

The Arab world is a diverse region with varied cultural practice. It is necessary to learn the culture of each Arab country to discover the opportunities available to your business. In doing so, you will face a culture that will overwhelm you with its pleasantness, generosity, and friendliness. Despite the negative portrayal of this region in the media and the associated negative image of war and terror, there is much more to these countries. They will surprise and amaze you.

The stereotypes listed in this book, which often cloud Western interpretations of Arab culture, offend many Arab people. It is very important that when you are dealing or talking with people from a specific Arab country, that you are careful when talking about differences within the Arab world. Coming from a different culture, it can also be hard to separate the differences in the Arab world. You may be unsure which country people come from or which tribes exist across several countries such as the GCC, Iraq and the Levant. The person you are talking to could easily feel insulted and lose confidence if you mentioned a tribe they belong to, even if you are talking about this tribe in another country.

Business and individuals visiting the Arab world or working with Arabs in or outside their countries at all levels must address cultural awareness as a key factor to reduce blunders that may lead to unexpected business failure. Culture knowledge must be an important pillar of any business strategy in the Arab world. In the Arab region, you should use culture to win business contracts and customers. Many projects fail because of clashing cultural differences and misunderstandings, and other projects stop before completion for the same reasons. The success of many businesses in the Arab world depends on the ability of their staff to interpret and adapt to Arab culture.

Anyone doing business in the Arab world must take the social and cultural dynamics of business proceedings very seriously and make a significant effort to build personal relationships with their counterparts. Arabs are part of what is called an 'honour culture.' This is quite different from Western culture. An 'honour culture' is when the action of one person affects everyone in the group, not only the individual, this means that both the person's and the group's reputation is affected. Therefore, opinions and reputations affect both the individual and their family; as I said previously, business relations are personal.

As I will explain later, for Arabs, business and personal are regarded as the same, so the time spent building a relationship is not wasted. Any attempt to accelerate this process will increase the chance of making a wrong decision when trying to do business or close a deal.

A Categorisation of the Arab Countries: Similarities and Differences

Arabs are not a racial group and include both black and white Arabs. Those who speak Arabic are often labelled as Arabs, but this is not also correct. For instance, Arabic-speaking Jews, Copts, and other minorities in the Arab world do not think of themselves as Arabs. In each part or region of the Arab world, different groups have their own traditions and different dialects, so it is not easy to distinguish an Arab just by their behaviour.

The Arab world includes some remarkably diverse countries. There are dramatic differences among the Arab countries. Some are very rich, others are desperately poor, and not as many Westerners think that all Arabs live in oil-rich countries. Indeed, there are huge wealth differences among Arab countries. The region is home to some of the richest economies in the world, such as the GCC countries, where you will meet Arab men and women who live in luxury. However, at the same time it is also home to some of the poorest, such as the extreme poverty in much of Yemen, Egypt, the Levant, and North Africa where, in some cases, people can't afford basic necessities. This demonstrates that the stereotype in the West that the Arabs are awash with oil is not correct.

In reality, most Arab countries have far less income than developed economies. Possibly no other region in the world is marked by such extreme disparities in wealth as the Arab region. Six countries (Comoros, Djibouti, Mauritania, Somalia, Sudan, and Yemen) that together represent a quarter of the region's population are classified as least developed by the United Nations and are among the poorest countries in the world. At the other end of the spectrum are Kuwait, Qatar, and the United Arab Emirates, which are among the world's wealthiest nations, as reflected in their per capita gross domestic product. *(Mirkin, 2010)*

What do "The GCC", "The Maghreb" and "The Levant" mean?

Gulf Cooperation Council- "GCC"

The Gulf Cooperation Council (GCC) is a political and economic alliance of six countries in the Arabian Peninsula: **Bahrain, Kuwait, Oman, Qatar, Saudi Arabia and the United Arab Emirates.** Established in 1981, the GCC promotes economic, security, cultural and social cooperation between the six states and holds a summit every year to discuss cooperation and regional affairs. *(Aljazeera, 2017)*

The GCC countries are home to more than 65 million people. The resource-rich region controls a substantial per cent of the world's oil reserves and natural gas reserves. The GCC has a very strong link to the West because of the predominance of oil, sold to the West. They also have a surplus of capital and some of the highest per capita income in the world. The member countries have very limited agriculture, and some have a small population. GCC countries tend to have a shortage of native skilled labour and rely on the Asian and Arab migrants from poorer countries to fill this gap.

It is important to highlight that many now believe that the GCC has become a broken organisation due to the complex relationships in 2017 between the UAE, Saudi, Bahrain, and Qatar. The council has undergone severe changes, however, over the past 4 years, the transformations have yet to fix the problems.

North Africa "The Maghreb" (Algeria, Morocco, Tunisia, Mauritania, and Libya)
The Maghreb is at the crossroads to Europe, Africa, and the Middle East, and has shared history, culture, and language in common. Recently it has attracted attention because of

the issues of refugees and illegal migrants entering Europe, etc. Stabilization of the political system and security situation is a crucial issue.

This group stretches from the Atlantic shores of Morocco in the West to the Red Sea in the East and is usually called Northern Africa. Some people say it only includes Morocco, Algeria, and Tunisia, which was ruled by the French during their colonial era.

Some of the countries in this group have nuclear uranium ore, and resources such as gold, and copper. Some are rich in oil and gas, such as Algeria and Libya, and others have massive natural resources and tourism, like Morocco and Tunisia. The region is full of promise and untapped resources - from minerals, land, and people's capital. However, many are yet to fully realise their potential with lower per capita income and a shortage of technical skills.

The French influence in these countries remains strong. French business practices still exist, and French is the primary language of communication and business rather than Arabic.

Nile Valley (Egypt and Sudan)

Despite their huge populations, these are very poor countries. Oil and the major natural resources, including significant deposits of chromium ore, copper, iron ore, mica, silver, and gold are the main industries in Sudan. Although there has been a greater development in agriculture, industry, and tourism in Egypt which are the main sources of income. However, Egypt has a shortage of capital and a very low per capita income.

Levant (Jordan, Lebanon, Syria, and Palestine)

These are also very poor countries, despite the close link with the West and the GCC. They rely on the service sector which is the most important economic sector but developed manufacturing, agriculture and tourism also play a big part in Lebanon and Jordan, these countries have a shortage of capital and a very low per capita income.

Others (Iraq, Yemen, Comoro Islands, Djibouti, and Somalia)

All of these countries live in critical situations due to war and other economic difficulties. Some of the countries in this group are rich in oil, like Iraq but its people live in very poor circumstances despite the great opportunities the country has. Yemen is sometimes considered to be part of the GCC because it is very close to the Arabian Peninsula, but Yemen has its own long history and culture and is part of the Horn of Africa. The Comoro Islands, Djibouti, and Somalia rest with no resources and they are very poor countries.

Arab Attitudes towards Westerners

The East & West Clash

Stereotypes fill a gap inside us whenever we meet anyone, Westerners can sometimes find the behaviour and attitudes of Arab counterparts puzzling, and in turn, Arab are occasionally offended or confused by Westerns way of looking at them. In reality, these misunderstandings create incorrect stereotypes on both sides.

Historically, Arabs and the West have had a very unpleasant relationship. History is very important for Arab people who are very history-aware and are convinced that the younger generations should always read and learn about the lessons and experience of their history and the actions of some Western countries that caused damage to their region, through colonization, and the unfair treaties.

Many Westerners see the Arab people as people who are jealous of the development and good things happening in the West. Many believe that Arabs are trying to act like Westerns or to be Westerns. Also, we cannot ignore that even though the image of Arabs and Muslims is misleading in Western media. In general, Arabs respect the Westerners latest achievements and their advancement in many levels, from education, technology, and the standard of living.

Arab media have given a negative image of Western politicians supporting attacks on Arabs and Muslims. As a result of the western military involvement and occupations and the long colonial control by the British and the French, the distorted image of Western men or women is as attackers, occupiers, or colonisers. As an Arab living in the west, it is easy for me to see that some of the Arab media across the world, particularly the religious ones, are involved in stereotyping Westerners as enemies of Arabs and Muslims.

The differences between the Arab countries when it comes to modernisation, wealth, and the Western approach and influences are quite big. As I mentioned before, in the GCC countries people have a very high standard of life which is almost a Western approach. At the same time, they also have a very conservative culture, beneath the Westernisation, these people remain heavily influenced by the teachings of Arab culture and Islam. When you start dealing with the Arabs you will meet some Arab business partners, customers, tourists, or students who are more Western than the "average" person in the West. Many of these Arabs are wealthy and have studied or who spent time in the West and visit it regularly. Even within each Arab country, you will find differences in how the West is received, for instance, large cities will have a more Western approach than those in more remote areas.

However, even those who might adopt Western behaviours or follow a Westerns way of living will always maintain their fundamental cultural manners. They live a Western-style life and enjoy its culture, but they do not accept Western influence in other parts of the same life, and they are very anti-West politically, particularly regarding the Western involvement in the Arab world. These people want to live in the Western world, but they do not want to be connected to what they believe is the loss of spirituality and an increase in materialism, loose sexual morality, a weakening of the family, and the downgrading of Arab history.

Divided by the West

The majority of Arabs blame the West, particularly Britain and France, for creating man-made states and separating their countries with borders to benefit their colonization. On May 19, 1916, representatives of Great Britain and France secretly reach an accord, known as the Sykes-Picot agreement, by which most of the Arab lands under the rule of the Ottoman Empire are to be divided into British and French spheres of influence with the conclusion of World War I. *(Connelly, 1978)*

You will find some Arabs still believe that the Westerners visiting their countries are people who do not respect or know anything about the Arab culture. They are seen as greedy, rude people with inappropriate behaviour and they only come to their countries to make money. Westerners are also often associated with the negativity associated with sex and drugs. Further clashes between Arabs and the West are also seen as a result of the political problems faced by many Arab countries over the past 70 years. These problems are often blamed on the earlier Western colonial policies. Moreover, many people in the Arab world see Western culture as a threat to traditional Islam and Arab culture values. There are also discussions and worries about the influence and attraction that Western values and cultural behaviours have on young Arab people.

Furthermore, many Arabs consider Westerners to be the main problem and reason for the war inside their countries. On the other hand, there are also Arabs, particularly from the upper and middle-class societies, who are fascinated by anything Western and try to live and act like them.

In recent years, many people in the Arab world have begun to believe that history is repeating itself, in terms of Western involvement in their region during the 20th and 21st centuries. They see this involvement as a repetition of the Crusades, when the Christian West started a very violent war on them, they also, see the Iraq war and the 'war against terror' as a continuation of that period.

Arab Loyalty: "Arabness"

It is very hard to predict who the Arabs are loyal to because of many factors. In terms of religion, there is a regional tension between the Sunnis and Shias. With regards to the cold war, there is also tension between Saudi Arabia and Iran. Tension also exists as a result of the huge numbers of Arab refugees from Syria, Yemen, Iraq, Libya, Somalia and other countries, the situation in Palestine and the harsh economy in Egypt, Jordan and Morocco, as well as the instability in Lebanon, Tunisia and Algeria, and the political tension between the GCC countries.

Despite this tension, many Arabs believe that themselves to be Arab and not belonging to a specific country. They believe that the separation with borders is temporary. This feeling was very strong in the past and mainly in countries like Syria, Iraq, Jordan, Yemen, Egypt, Libya, Tunisia, and Algeria, now this feeling is declining and many of them are now thinking about how to create a better future for themselves.

TRUST ME,
I'M
عربي

The New Generations & Cultural Change

The Changing Face of Arab Culture

The Arab world is being transformed by conflicts and wars. However, it is also being transformed by a new generation of men and women who are fighting to live a life of dignity, both in politics and business. Children and young people (0-24 year olds) in the Middle East and North Africa currently account for nearly half of the region's population and have the potential to become agents of change, acting for a more prosperous and stable future for themselves and their communities, and playing their part in reaping the demographic dividend *(UNICEF, 2019)*, making it one of the world's most youthful markets and regions in the world. Many in the Arab world consider education to be the most effective tool to do this. Across the Arab world, students are under pressure in education, socially and culturally. Many parents want their children to do well at school and university as they see the education of their children as a great honour. Currently, thousands of Arab students of both genders complete their education and higher education in the West and other parts of the world. A large number of students and education development has created a massive growth of new middle-class people. A by-product of this is changing in family, children, and women's place in the society which has caused a new conflict between the educated, young, and middle class with some of the older traditional social customs. The new economics, educational levels, and technology have opened the way for many strict cultural rules to change, such as the social interactions between men and women in all aspects of life.

In recent years, many of the solid social barriers in Arab culture have changed, the region is going through 'uncontrolled' changes. More than half the young people in much of the Arab world would like to leave their home countries, a survey conducted by BBC Arabic has found. That number has jumped by more than 10 per cent for those aged 18-29 since 2016, according to the Big BBC News Arabic Survey 2018/19, conducted with the Arab Barometer research group. The survey received responses from more than 25,000 people aged 18 and over in Morocco, Algeria, Tunisia, Libya, Egypt, Palestine, Yemen, Jordan, Iraq, Sudan, and Lebanon *(Arab Barometer 2019)*.

When doing business with the Arabs, you will meet two types of people, the younger generation who are well-educated and Westernised who introduce new modernisation and changes to their culture, and those people who want the Islamic conservative rules to remain, while modernising Arab culture. This means that there is great variability in how Arabs act, with some acting more stereotypically and others not. You may even be able to carry out a Western-style of business with some people. However, be careful not to assume this is the case for everyone, even those who want a more modern culture. Whenever you speak or listen to the majority of Arabs, they will tell you that they do not want to replace Islam and the culture, as religion is part of their identity. However, they want to renew the way people look at the religion and understand it. "Young Arabs say religion plays too big of a role in the middle east and religious institutions need to be reformed" *(Asda'a Bcw 2019)*.

On the other hand, many of the conservative people, the old officials and business generation are still very conservative in their approach. In the Arab world these people, old and young, male and female, want to maintain the cultural and religious practice and the way of life and believe that they do not have to change their religion and culture to suit modernisations. They believe that any changes should always go with the religion and that Islam and Arab culture contributed and will contribute to the new world in the same way the new world can contribute to their life.

There is massive cultural and social development in the Arab world. Increased education, modernisation, Westernisation and the new middle-class have altered some Arab customs and traditions, such as lifestyle, family size and the empowerment of women. Women can now have a role in the economy and many other positions in society and business.

When you deal with Arabs or visit the Arab world, it remains important, however, to remember that many aspects of Arab culture and traditional values remain strong. The Arab world is still very conservative. Many of the changes mentioned have not changed the culture. Values including religion, family, honour, shame, respect, hospitality, and generosity are still part of all Arabs, they are becoming modernised, but they are not becoming Western.

TRUST ME,
I'M
عربي

5 The Arab Contribution to Civilisation

Arabic and Islamic Influence on Western Culture

"A Good Read"

Bringing History to Life

For centuries, Arabic was used by European scholars to advance their knowledge and teaching, especially after the collapse of the Roman Empire. Like other cultures, Arabs have made many contributions to our civilisations throughout history. Arab culture is rich in music, art, mathematics, geography, medicine, astronomy, and architecture. Some of the oldest literature cultures exist in the Arab world and the tradition of Arabic literature stretches back some 16 centuries to unrecorded beginnings in the Arabian Peninsula. At certain points in the development of European civilisation, the literary culture of Islam and its Arabic medium of expression came to be regarded not only as models for emulation but also, through vital conduits as direct sources of inspiration for the intellectual communities of Europe, such as Moorish Spain and Norman Sicily.

The oldest existing and continually operating educational institution in the world is the University of Karueein, founded in 859 AD in Fez, Morocco. The University of Bologna, Italy, was founded in 1088 and is the oldest one in Europe (Grau. 2018).

During the Dark Ages, the Arab Empire had its Golden Age. This period saw Arabian impact and achievements in many fields, including astronomy, medicine, mathematics, philosophy and many more. The developments occurred out of the Arabian advancements and from translations of their texts into Greek, especially in the 9th century. Muslim scholars knew of many books written, not only by ancient Greek and Roman writers but by Persian, Indian and Chinese writers too. A famous caliph, al-Mamun, set up a translating house in Baghdad which translated the books from all these countries into Arabic. Later on, in the 11th century, in Toledo, Spain; these Arabic editions were translated into Latin and circulated all over Christian Europe (BBC).

Many European universities translated a large part of the medicine, science and philosophy texts from Arabic and used it for knowledge advancement and teaching for centuries. For instance, currently, the Indo-Arabic numerals (0-9), affect everything in our daily lives from business to education and the marketplace. They replaced Roman numerals which were discovered by the Muslim academic, Al-Khwarizmi.

The linguistic research of the first two Islamic centuries laid the foundations for a new universal culture of science. Of particular relevance to the later development of science were the extensive compilation efforts by Arabic philologists and lexicographers *(Ansari and Nawwab 2016)*.

Another important contribution to the advancement of civilisation was in the fields of health and medicine. Did you know that the first hospitals occurred in the Arab cities like Baghdad, Cairo, and Damascus hundreds of years before hospitals are known to be used in Europe? During the Islamic and Arabic empire, the world saw some great developments in medicine which were written in Arabic and used as a great motivation for other cultures who borrow from the Arab culture. From the 10th century until the 17th century medicine of the Islamic and Arabic empire was one of the main references for medicine in Europe. For almost 500 years, a huge medical encyclopaedia known as "Al-Canon of Medicine" written by Ibn Sina (also known as Avicenna) was taught across universities in Europe and was used as the medical textbook for European doctors.

The universities in Europe at Montpelier in France and Salerno in Italy pursued the help of Arabian universities in Al-Andalus. Many of European philosophers used the Arabic novel, Hayy ibn Yaqzan, as a reference for their work. It was penned by a 12th-century Arab intellectual, Ibn Tufayl and published in Oxford. In music, the first written notes in Western classical music were written in Arab Spain.

So many aspects of our daily lives today were influenced by Muslims and Arabs contributions. The peoples' influence, culture, and history of the Arabs remain significantly anonymous to most people in the West even when we talk about long interaction between both regions.

*Arab's are extremely proud of their heritage. It is advisable to
learn a little about Arabic heritage so that you can use it in conversation.
Discourse such as this may cause your business relationship to develop positively.*

TRUST ME,
I'M

عربي

6

Islam

A critical Factor for Success in the Arab World

Business Influences Culture

Religion Influences Culture

What is Islam?

Islam is an Arabic word derived from the word peace. It also means to submit to a higher will or seeking peace by submitting to the "divine will". Islam is the second-largest faith, with 1.6 billion followers globally.

Understanding Islam

To understand the Arab people and how they behave or act you must understand Islam. Religion in the Arab world affects every aspect of their life. Islam is part of every part of a Muslim's life and influences how they interact with one another. For Arabs, Islam is not only culturally important but also in how they live their life including how they do business. It can be a sensitive subject which may offend. It is very hard to overcome any mistakes associated with religion in the Arab world.

Who are the Muslims?

Muslims are individuals who completely and peacefully submit to the will of God, believe in the articles of Faith, and practice the five pillars of Islam. They worship the One God and revere Prophet Muhammad as the last messenger of God, they also believe in all the prophets which preceded the Prophet Muhammad. Non-Muslim can become a Muslim simply by saying "There is no god but God, and Muhammad is the Messenger of God" which is called the declaration of faith the "Shahadah" in Arabic *(Esposito 2011)*.

In Arabic, Allah simply means 'God'. The Quran, the Hadith , and the whole Islamic tradition maintain that the God of the Jews, the Christians, and the Muslims is the same God. Arabic-speaking Muslims cannot imagine using a different word than "Allah" when referring to the God worshipped by Christians and Jews. Arabic-speaking Christians and Jews themselves worship God using the word "Allah" *(Ansari and Nawwab 2016)*.

What is Quran?

Quran is the holy book for Muslims. The Qur'an is the holy book for Muslims, revealed in stages to the Prophet Muhammad over 23 years. Qur'anic revelations are regarded by Muslims as the sacred word of God, intended to correct any errors in previous holy books such as the Old and New Testaments *(Marco 2019)*. It is a record of the exact words revealed by God through the Angel Gabriel to the prophet Muhammad. Muslims believe that not one word of the 114 chapters has changed over 14 centuries. The Quran is the main reference and source for how Muslim behave, worship, and practise their religion and their day-to-day life.

What's Sharia Law?

Sharia law is the umbrella for Islamic practice. The Sharia is simply the body of law, rules, and regulations of Islam. The Sharia covers everything in a Muslim's life, including business. What is allowed and not allowed is very important in Islam and, therefore, almost everything in life comes under it. For example, alcohol and gambling, are sinful and not allowed. This means that Muslims should not use it or do business with it (although you will still find some Arabs and Muslims, investing in doing business in these industries).

What's Halal & Haram?

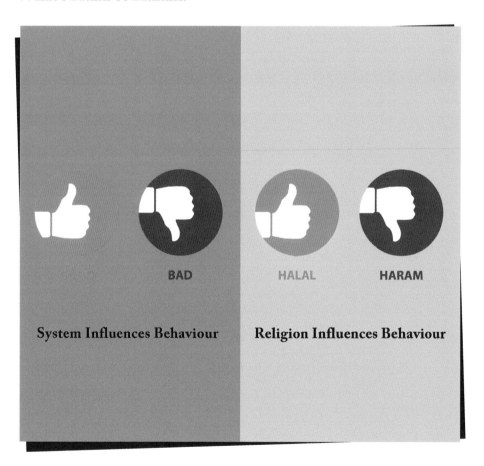

Everything in Islam is based on Halal and Haram, business is no exception. Halal means lawful or permissible. In the West, many think of it as a reference to food and what can be eaten, but in fact, it is a way of life. The opposite of Halal is Haram. This means something is forbidden or unlawful. The ethics of what is Halal and Haram were set down in what is known as Sharia Law, which is based primarily on the Quran and the Hadith. Business and companies pursuing to enter the Arab world must ensure that all their product complies with the halal guidelines for all Arab markets. Remember, Halal and Haram are different from one Arab country to another.

The Five Pillars of Islam

In Islam, there are five "Pillars of the Faith", the Declaration of faith in God "Shahadah", Prayer "Salat", Fasting "Sawm", Pilgrimage "Hajj" and Charity giving "Zakat". These pillars are the five principal duties that are obligatory for Muslims of all backgrounds and all different sects of Islam. I will talk about them briefly because of their likely effects on your Arab business counterparts and the way they do business.

The Declaration of Faith in God the "Shahadah"

The belief that "There is no god but God, and Muhammad is the Messenger of God" is central to Islam. This phrase, written in Arabic, is often prominently featured in architecture and a range of objects, including the Quran. One becomes a Muslim by reciting this phrase with conviction.

In the Arab world, you will hear the name of "Allah" in almost everything Arabs do, in conversation, going to the shop, counting money, and eating. Speeches and letters start with, "In the name of God, Most Gracious, Most Merciful."

Islam is not just a way to educate Muslims, it is how they should live their life.

Prayer "Salat"

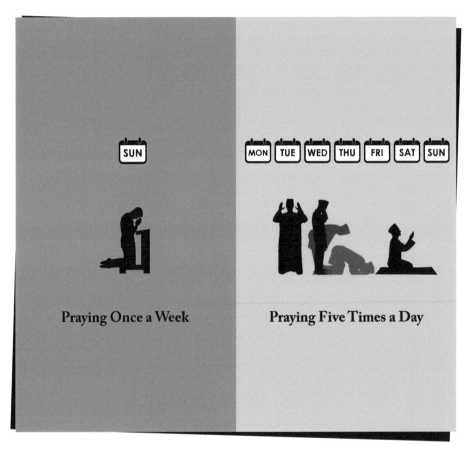

Praying Once a Week   **Praying Five Times a Day**

The second pillar of Islam is prayer. Prayer is one of the most apparent influences of Islam. Unlike the West, praying occurs not once a week, but five times a day, at certain times and in different physical positions. Muslims pray facing Mecca five times a day; at dawn, noon, mid-afternoon, sunset, and after dark. Prayer performed on a small rug or mat used expressly for this purpose. Muslims can pray individually at any location or together in a mosque.

Praying is different from one country to another and is dependent on where you are in the Arab world; not all the Arabs go to the mosque. Some pray at home or in the office and some do not pray at all. You might meet a business counterpart in some part of the Arab world, where you have to tailor your meeting around prayer time. Friday is the holy day for Muslims and the midday prayers are obligatory for all males to attend.

The call to Prayer

In the Arab world, you will hear the call to prayer five times a day, not only in mosques but also in airports, universities, and government buildings. Prayers take place just before dawn, and at midday, late afternoon, sunset and night. The exact time of prayers is usually printed in the local newspapers and can be found in English.

I have witnessed on several occasions when in the Arab world with Westerns, that they have some very mixed reactions when they talk about being woken up by the loudspeakers of mosque's "call to prayer" at 3 am, for example. Some might enjoy the experience and there are even videos online showing Westerners enjoying or getting irritated by the call to prayer in malls in UAE or elsewhere. However, no matter how you feel about the call to prayer, it is essential that you never complain about it. If you did so, you would cause great offence.

Fasting "Sawm" (The Month of Ramadan)

The third Pillar is Fasting (Ramadan) is another aspect of Islam that Westerners visiting or living in an Arab country may need to get used to. Ramadan is fasting from dawn until sunset, this includes no eating, drinking, or smoking. You will find business hours are reduced and people are more relaxed. A friend once told me that Ramadan is the time of the year when everything is upside down and it is really hard to do business. The month of Ramadan is a very special time for the Arabs and Muslims, and it is also considered to be a great time to visit people and enjoy the late-night atmosphere. Therefore, if you are in an Arab country for business during Ramadan, go out at night and enjoy the atmosphere, Arabs love to socialise during nighttime in Ramadan and stay up late until the early hours of the morning. I know of many contracts that were signed because of the friendly approach from a Westerner during the Ramadan nights atmosphere and the late gatherings with their Arabs partners. It is important to remember that, in some parts of the Arab world, it is very strict when it comes to Westerners eating during the day of Ramadan. If you do happen to be in an Arab country during Ramadan, it is polite to eat, drink, and smoke inside and away from the public eye.

Charity Giving "Zakat"

The fourth Pillar is Zakat or almsgiving. In accordance with Islamic law, all Muslims who meet the necessary criteria to donate a fixed portion of their income to community members in need and to charitable causes. Many rulers and wealthy Muslims build mosques, hospitals, schools, and other institutions both as a religious duty and to secure the blessings associated with charity.

Zakat is based on income and the value of possessions, which is 2.5%, or 1/40 of a Muslim's total savings and wealth.

Pilgrimage "Hajj"

The fifth Pillar is the pilgrimage "Hajj" Every Muslim whose health and finances permit it must make at least one visit to the holy city of Mecca, in present-day Saudi Arabia. Muslims believe that it is the house Abraham "Ibrahim in Arabic" built for God, and face in its direction "Qebla" when they pray. Since the time of the Prophet Muhammad, believers from all over the world have gathered around the "the Ka'ba" (the point of orientation for Muslims when they pray, and it is also the focal point of the Pilgrimage). on the eighth and twelfth days of the final month of the Islamic calendar. This is not obligatory if a person is not able to do it, such as for sickness of financial reasons. (If they can, all Muslims have to make the journey at least once in their lifetime).

Islamic Holidays

The Two Eid

There are two main festivals you should be aware of when in the Arab world. Eid Al-Fitr occurs just after Ramadan and Eid Al-Adha occurs after the annual pilgrimage. Holidays around both Eids are usually for three days but it is normal for the governments to extend it. It is wise to avoid doing business on or near the two Eids.

Friday

The holy day for Muslims is Friday. Muslims believe that the "Day of Judgment" will take place on Friday. Men gather in the mosque for the noonday prayer on Friday; women can do but not obliged to participate. After the prayer, a sermon "Khutba in Arabic" focuses on a passage from the Quran, followed by prayers by the "Imam" and a discussion of a particular religious' topic. When in the Arab world you will hear the "Imam" give the Friday sermon "Khutba" through loudspeakers. At the time of prayer, roads will be busy or even blocked if you live close to a mosque.

How Religious are Arabs?

It is not easy to answer the extent people are religious because what religion is to one individual is completely something different to another. A recent *(BBC, 2019)* survey "The Arab world in seven charts: Are Arabs turning their backs on religion?" of the Arab world found that 'religiosity' had dropped among Arabs. Yet, Islam remains the shaping factor in Arab life and culture.

Religion is worshipped in different ways by different people. From Morocco to Yemen, across North Africa, The Levant and The GCC, Islam is practised and interpreted differently. Like other major religions, there are significant, historic disagreements between different sects.

Moreover, the rule of the religion is not as strict for all Arab people. For example, Alcohol is "Haram". However, some Arabs will drink openly and have a good knowledge of alcohol, sometimes more than the Westerns themselves.

Other Arabic Religions

Arabs are very diverse religiously. While the majority are Muslims, there are also numbers of Christians in Jordan, Egypt, Lebanon, Syria, Palestine, and Iraq and Jews in Morocco, Bahrain, Tunisia, and Yemen. Other religious and minority groups exist in the majority of Arab countries. Muslims acknowledge Jews and Christians as the "People of the Book," "Ahl Al-kitab" the Bible, and believe their one god is the same for both Jews and Christians. The Islamic law allows the survival of both Jews and Christians during historical cultural and religious troubles. However, Muslim also believe that the messages for both religions were misinterpreted. They also believe that Prophet Muhammad is the restorer of the old faith of Adam, Abraham.

Despite there being multiple faiths in the Arab world, Islam governs all aspect of Arab life. When visiting an Arabic country, you will find that Islam influences everything; when you shop, walk in the street and most importantly, when you do business. It is important to know the influence of Islam before doing business in the Arab world. Such knowledge will decrease the chance of cultural and religious blunders and aid to know you during business meetings and negotiations. Your understanding of Islam will help you to expect its influence and impact on daily and commercial life.

Your awareness the religion practices is most important. "Halal and Haram", Prayer and its times, Ramadan, Sharia Law, and other aspects of Islam will have an important impact on your business practice and your counterpart will value that you are respecting their beliefs and customs. So, if you are planning to do business in the Arab world, it is important to have a good understanding of this religion so that you do not make any mistakes.

Christianity and Christians in the Arab world:

Arab Christians and Eastern Christians

There are two types of Christians in the Arab world, some are very proud of being Arab, the Arab Christians, and other Christians see Arabs as foreigners who should not be in their countries, the Eastern Christians.

The Eastern Christians believe that they have nothing in common with Islam and want to distance their heritage from anything Islamic or Arabic. Like the Egyptians Christians, they believe they are descendants of the ancient Egyptians and see the Arab Muslims as invaders of their country. There are also divided Christians in Lebanon, who believe they are not Arab, but descendants of the Phoenicians. They believe that they are more rooted in their region than the Arabs. The other Lebanese Christians believe that they are Arabs Christians. Also, Christians in Iraq and some of the Syrian Christians believe they are the oldest Christians on earth and, in some part of Syria Aramaic, "Jesus language" is still spoken.

The Arab Christians in Jordan, Palestine, and a large part of Syria, have a positive relationship with Islam and have no problem being part of the Islamic civilisation. They believe that they are Arab and many of them fight for Arab nationalism and share the anti-Western movement towards their region.

What do Muslims think About Jesus?

Arabs and Muslim's in general respect and revere Jesus, they believe he will come back and await his second coming. They also believe that he is one of the greatest prophets, although they will never refer to him as Jesus (ISSA in Arabic), they will use, instead, the phrase "peace be upon him". Mary is considered the purest woman of all creation.

Christian Holidays

Some Arab countries have significant Christian populations. Therefore, you can expect Christian holidays like Christmas and Easter to also affect days of business.

What's Your Religion?

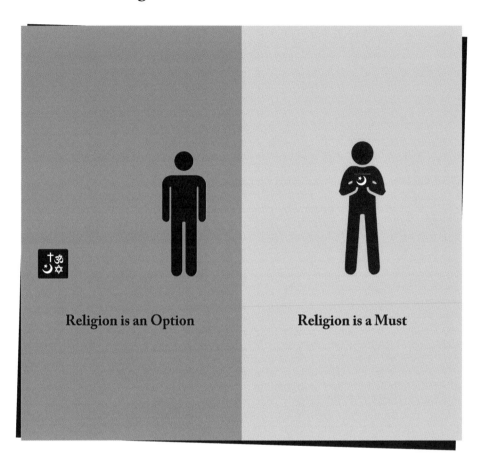

It is normal for your conversation with an Arab to turn to religion or politics at any point. So, do not be surprised if you are asked 'What is your religion?' This is not rude; it is just honest interest. For a Westerner, religion is a private matter, however, this is not the case for Arabs so be ready to be asked and prepare yourself to answer the question.

It is okay to say that you are Christian or Jewish. Arabs love to talk to you about what your religion and Islam share in common. They enjoy discussing religion with Westerners because of their curiosity about Western religious beliefs and because they feel motivated to share information about Islam with friends as a favour to them. As I mentioned before, Christians and Jews are respected as 'people of the book', who share the same God. It is important to remember not to criticise Islam and never say that you are an atheist.

7 Family Life

Keeping it in the Family

Family Always First

As I mentioned before, culture and religion are a key part of Arab behaviours and affect how Westerns should interact with them. Besides Islam, the family is the second most important element in the Arab world. Loyalty to your family is important above all else and family obligations can affect both personal and business aspects of life.

The role of family and hierarchy in the Arab world can be of much confusion for Westerners. The same confusion can be found in business and society as a whole. The family plays a central role in decision making, such decisions are often more individual in the West, such as a suitable career and whom to marry. In some cases, for example, if a member of a family murders someone from another family, the entire family could be punished and suffer the consequences of the action of the individual.

Family Structure

In Arab families, the head of the family, usually the eldest male, holds a supreme position in the family. They are responsible for the behaviour of the entire family. The most senior female will also have an almost equal position. All other members of the family must respect this structure and the positions within the family hierarchy. The head of the family instructs all members who follow his orders, out of respect and responsibility. Younger male respect older males as much as younger females will respect older female's sister. It is regarded as a sign of rudeness and a bad family if a member of a family argues. Each member of the family knows the other member's relationship, the oldest as address as "Elder Daughter", or "Elder Brother" and the same for the younger ones, and using these names is a most likely way to enforce the importance of the family relationships.

Of course, family among many other things and culture, in general, are changing in the Arab world. The new modernisation, political, economic, and social development changed the structure of the family causing many families to adapt to a new way of life with new values. However, the cultural values of a family are still respected, and family remains an important part of Arab culture.

"I and my brothers against my cousins; I and my cousins against the strangers."
This popular saying among the Arabs should explain family importance.

Respect

Another aspect of Arab culture closely connected to family is respect. Children are taught to show respect to their parents, grandparents, and older family members. The respect value must be seen and adhered to in and outside the family. Even senior persons (a crown prince or a very influential person) still kiss their fathers' or mothers' hands and heads whenever they see them after a few days being away, to show great respect in both the privacy of the home and in public.

One of the measures of a good family is for its members to show respect to older family members. This is also relevant to younger members of society, who must be respectful to anyone older. Children must speak politely to strangers and refer to anyone older as uncle or aunt. Respect is also determined in classes of society, ranks and positions from the top-down, for officials, people with authority or any position in society.

Arab Family Business

Family and its considerations and principles are important when you do business in the Arab world, because creating trust and working relationships are centred around families, Business leaders use their power to ensure that their family members come first. This kind of family relationship means that it is easier to develop trust in business relationships. It will open the door to rewarding business opportunities that will be locked to others who do not have the connections and relations through the family.

The majority of Arab businesses are family owned. Big business is owned by families in the Arab world mainly GCC, and leadership is centred in the family with family members, with succession running in the family. In the GCC, most of the businesses are multi-generational family groups, and it is very common that the head of the company is one of the eldest in the family and is highly respected. Decision-making often only occurs within a small group of directors around him. It is, therefore, important to know the structure of the business you are dealing with. It is common for the big companies in the GCC to have a large number of senior expatriates (mainly Westerners). Their job is mainly to assess you and what you are offering before they present it to the family decision-makers. A large number of lower managerial positions, mostly in the GCC countries, are also filled by expatriates, mainly from South Asian countries (Indians and Pakistanis), but also from other Arab countries, such as Egypt, Lebanon, Palestine, Jordan, Syria, and North Africa.

Family matters can always influence Arabic behaviour in business. In many cases, disagreement within the family will affect external relationships which could affect your business if you are in the middle of a deal. When doing business, always remember, Arab businesses are often family-owned and Arab families are very large and very close. Be careful not to talk negatively about someone as they may be a family member. The important rule in the Arab world is that everyone knows everyone, any negative words or comments from you will reach the person concerned quicker than you expect.

To Arabs, information about their family, friends and close connections is important, even more important than the information about themselves. They use the family to define anyone they meet, such as their social status and connections without knowing the person himself. Therefore, they share more information about themselves than Westerners might do. They enjoy a lot of self-praise and praise of their relatives and it is normal for some Arabs to give details of whom they know and their social connections in government or high places. When they share this information about their influence network which could be very useful for your business, particularly if you are ever in need of high-level personal contacts. You may be expected to give more personal and family information, as well as information about your work, experience, and education.

Are we Friends?

When with the Arabs, you will always hear them mentioning that you are a friend, even after a few meetings, but do not take it as it is. It may be a form of politeness. However, if you work on developing a real friendship with them, which is the wise thing to do, and with their friendship, then your job will be much easier. Although, you can not rely on that alone for your business success.

TRUST ME,
I'M

عربي

8 Language

Do you know how many Arabic Words there are for Love?

*"At least 11 words, each of them conveys
a different way of falling in love"*

The Arabic language creates an impression everywhere it is spoken. Some find it attractive and polite; others find it intense, and many others see it as a challenge. Arabic has an incredible identity, as well as an epic history. The Arabic language was a primary tool that contributed to the integration and cultural coherence of the Islamic empire. As one of the most distinctive highlights of Islamic culture, Arabic rapidly became the lingua franca of a vast, unified empire. Already before the rise of Islam, Arabic was the primary form of cultural production amongst the Arabs *(Ansari and Nawwab 2016)*.

Arabic connects the people across the Arab world, uniting many different ethnic groups, religious communities, and nationalities. There are more than 500 million Arabic speakers across the world, Arabic is one of the most widely spoken languages globally and it is the religious language used by more than 1.6 billion Muslims. Many other faiths use Arab for their liturgy and prayers in the Arab world, such as Christians.

It is one of the official languages of the United Nations and has been identified by The British Council, as the second most important language for the UK's future *(British Council 2017)*. It is the fourth-most widely spoken language in the world after Mandarin, English, and Spanish. Many words commonly used in English have Arabic roots such as alcohol, cotton, magazine, safari, coffee, and many others.

Arabic is also a very powerful religious language. Arabs are proud of their mother tongue. However, the spoken Arabic varies from one country to another, although classical Arabic has remained the same for centuries. It is believed that it is the language of God; 'language of heaven'; the language will be spoken in heaven.

Is there more than one Arabic?

The language has two types:

Classical Arabic: This is the language you will read in books and newspapers and hear on the news; this is the same across the whole Arab world. However, it is almost impossible to find anybody who wants to talk to you in Classical Arabic. When foreigners who have learnt the language at universities start to speak the classical language with a local, they find it strange and the local may feel impressed. That is because many native Arabic speakers think 'Modern Standard Arabic' sounds overly formal and old-fashioned.

Colloquial Arabic: You will hear this in regular conversation. Each Arabic country has a distinct accent and, in some cases, its own dialect. The GCC countries share a very close and similar dialect. The North African Arab countries (also known as the Arab Maghreb) share a similar dialect. The Levant also has a similar dialect. Egypt, Iraq, and the rest of the Arab world, each have their different and distinct dialects. It is important to mention that, because of the influence of the Egyptian media which is widely watched and loved throughout the Arabic-speaking world, the Egyptian accent is understood in every Arabic country. In the past decade, the Syrian and GCC drama and TV programs were widely watched and the Lebanese and Iraqi songs are popular all over the Arab world. This makes their accent understood in North Africa for example and that is because of the media influence, not because Arab understand all accents.

I will highlight some of the regions and languages of Arab countries:

Egyptian Arabic: The Egyptian dialect is the most universally understood by Arabs throughout the region, given the influence of Egyptian music and films in Arabic media. Egyptian Arabic is spoken in Egypt and some part of Sudan. It differs a lot to modern standard Arabic.

North African "Maghrebi" Arabic: Maghrebi Arabic is spoken in North Africa (Algeria, Libya, Mauritania, Morocco, Tunisia). Their dialects are very difficult to understand by other Arabic speakers. Their dialects and accent are extremely original and unique in sound! However, they can understand most other accents, mainly because of the media influence and their attractions to the Middle Eastern songs and TV programs.

Levantine Arabic: Levantine Arabic is spoken in Jordan, Syria, Lebanon, and Palestine. It is one of the most popular choices for new Westerns learners, besides Egyptian Arabic, due to its amusing, tuneful sound.

Gulf and Iraqi Arabic: The gulf Arabic is the strongest delicate and has more of a Bedouin-style (Saudi, UAE, Qatar, Kuwait, Oman, Bahrain, and Iraq). It was rarely heard outside the GCC countries in the past, however, now with social media and the influence of the songs and the GCC media power, you will hear it in songs and TV programs all over the Arab world.

TRUST ME,
I'M
عربي

9 Arab Women

Misconceptions and Distorted Histories

As the CEO of the Arab Women of the Year Awards, the subject of the women of the Arab world is close to me. In the West, very often people asked me about the reforms and what Arab women are doing to play their part in building their communities. In my position, I have lost track of how often I have had to respond to questions about women's rights and female empowerment in the Arab world. You will be surprised to know that many Arab women have privileged positions in many ways and are treated with a great deal of respect, someone could say that, in some cases, more than in many Western countries.

In general, problems facing Arab women are often lost. according to the World Bank collection of development indicators, Arab women and girls made up 51% of the population in the Arab world. *(World Bank, 2019).* The position of Arab women in the Arab world varies extensively, it is wrong to apply the model of one country onto the whole Arab World.

Most Westerners believe that Arab women are oppressed and subservient to men. It is very easy to notice that in the West, Arab women are seen as victims of a negative Western stereotype which is often reflected in the Western media. It is often assumed that the severe conditions they see in the news, represent the standard for women throughout the Arab world. The symbol of Arab women is always seen as veiled females have now become the symbol of Arab and Muslim women in westerns media. This image is very upsetting to many Arab and Muslim women. Of course, I am not saying that a veil does not exist in the Arab world, and an increasing number of women wear it, but this is not the only image of women in the Arab world. In many cases, in documentaries and news programmes about the Arab world in general and Arab women in particular, extreme views take priority while moderate views are presented less or completely ignored.

Arab men are accused of being oppressors when it comes to the subject of women. Westerners are supportive of female empowerment, and for many Arab people, there remains a common question; why do you use Western women only as an example? Western women can be used as an example of the amazing achievements of women. However, you will also see incredible achievements for non-Western women, who are creating opportunities and shaping their communities and the world.

In the case of Arab women, a lack of knowledge of their history has resulted in narrow ideas about them by the West; thousands of years before Western women gained rights, Arab women began their liberation, and women had their own businesses and a role in their society. "The Islamic world housed some of the first and most advanced hospitals from the 8th century, Muslim female doctors and nurses were skilled and knowledgeable. Wounded crusaders preferred to go to a Muslim doctor than a Christian one because they were more knowledgeable" *(BBC)*. Even in recent years' women have played a big part in the liberation of their nations, such as in Algeria, Syria, and Egypt.

Of course, not everything is perfect for Arab women. There is no denying that some Arab women still have difficulty gaining access to education and health care. Some face threats to their safety and are forced into an early marriage, or made victims of gender-based violence, including the so-called "honour crimes". However, millions of Arab women still do the best they can with what they have and have shown remarkable tenacity and resilience to this effect. During the Arab history, the women's position has had its ups and downs. Nowadays, Arab women understand that they need to keep going, and at the same time, they still hold the culture deep inside them and understand that keeping their culture will not stop them from going far. I personally believe that women in the Arab world can contribute positively to their societies and use their knowledge in their life to advance society at large and be the new change.

Is it Religion or Culture?

The conservative nature of Arab society applies, play a big part in what is appropriate and what is not when it comes to women, for both Muslims and non-Muslims in the Arab world, including Christians in some Arab countries. Christians and other minorities share almost the same conservative attitudes as the Muslims in the region, and often it is hard to identify a religion by the clothes a person is wearing.

Many Arab women wear a headscarf and dress in clothes that do not reveal much skin. The conservative nature of the culture means that public displays of affection are not appreciated.

The issues around women in Arab countries is not just a simple religious issue. To understand the status of women in the Arab world, you must understand the link between religion and culture.

You might come across some very open and Westernised women in the Arab world. However, if you get to know them well, you will find that it is impossible to separate the influences of culture, family, and religion from how they behave. Therefore, to come closer to understanding the situation of women in the Arab world, you cannot separate culture and religion since they are attached. Arab culture is heavily influenced by different versions of strict interpretations of Islam and sometimes it is impossible to see the line that separates influence from the tribal culture and shame and honour from the religious teaching.

No one can deny that some conservative Arabs still view women working or studying in a gender-mixed environment as damage to their shame and honour. They blame this on religion, but I believe it is more cultural than religious. It is very hard to understand and deal with this mind-set. However, it is important to remember that, in the Arab world, while much of this comes from tradition, religion is often used to justify the traditions around values such as honour.

I believe that this is an obvious issue concerning Arab women. It is influenced by many different factors including culture, government (Politics), religious understanding and interpretations and tribal codes (Shame & Honour). It is easy to see the impact of all of this, even though Arab governments have given women more rights, culture, religion, and other factors in the Arab world will have a say in these changes and dictate its validity. Religion cannot be solely blamed for the women problem in the Arab world. It is obvious that the culture not religion has been the main barrier for women. This is why I believe any real change must come from the culture itself.

Furthermore, many of the steps taken by governments across the Arab world towards female empowerment and female advancement need substantial internal reforms and cannot be used for scoring international points in their diplomacy record. Yes, recent changes have helped women in many ways, however, it is clear that a change in law does not mean a change in mind-set.

Arab Women are making political changes in the region. In most Arab countries, women now have higher educational qualifications than men, and many are in senior positions in big companies. On top of social and economic progress, Arab women are making important steps in changing social attitudes on gender equality. The changes in the region are a credit to the great work of Arab women themselves. There is a major shift and changing mindsets in the region regarding gender equality, including access to education, employment, and political representation. I believe that more work is needed to improve women's rights. It must go beyond asking for equal rights towards a focus on the change of attitudes from society and what they can do to improve their lives and the lives of others around them.

Arab Women in the Business World

Many Arab women are well educated from a young age and think for themselves as creating their success, including those in the most conservative countries. People will argue that Arab women are not free to wear what they want, work with whomever they like or to behave freely outside their household. Whilst this is correct in some part of the Arab world, this does not mean they are treated any less in a large part of the Arab world, including the business environment. In fact, in the Arab world, you will find many women are highly respected and will be working alongside key male players. In many cases, you will be dealing with women as the decision-makers for your business.

Diversity exists among how women are treated from one Arab country to another. As previously mentioned, the rules of society still apply and determine what is appropriate behaviour and what is not. This does not mean you cannot do business with women; however, you shouldn't assume that she is in a senior position and wearing designer clothes and if she looks like a Westerner that behaves like a Western businesswoman. It is very important that you are not deceived by their external appearance. Arab woman's honour and her family's honour is based on her behaviour, and almost all women in the Arab world are proud of protecting that honour and respecting the culture and its tradition. Therefore, for the majority, this is not enforced on them, although there are still some cases where women do not have the option to choose their future.

TRUST ME,
I'M

عربي

Hospitality in the Arab World

Food, Friendship & Business

My Food   Our Food

Accept the Invitations

Hospitality and generosity are cultural values shared by all Arabs. Entertainment is part of their way of doing business and when in the Arab world, you should expect regular invitations, including food, drinks, lavish entertainment functions, and luxury gifts as part of their business culture and engagement with people, be ready for that.

Being a good and generous host is a serious thing for the Arabs. When Arabs offer you hospitality, is something they take very seriously. They feel that they must offer it as part of their culture; good hospitality is a big factor of their honour. However, many Westerners confuse it with business success, they take hospitality as a sign of deal success, whereas in some cases, this might be the opposite. If a contract is about to be lost and meetings are not succeeding, this could be used to say sorry.

What you need to know is that, if they invite you to their home, they want you to enjoy your time. Also, they want to know more about you and what you can contribute to their business because, for them, business is about connecting with others on a personal level. Hospitality is very important to Arabs and so it is essential that you always accept an invitation unless you have a very good reason not to do so, such as a travel arrangement or a family obligation. If you decline their invitation without a good reason, it is interpreted as a sign that you are not interested in their company or in building a relationship with them. As a relationship culture, this will affect your business. You must remember that an invitation to your counterpart's home is an opportunity to build friendship, a friendship that is essential for your business.

When at their home, arrive on time, but bear in mind you will eat late. Arab people love to talk and socialise before the food is served, and they will expect you to stay after the food is finished for more talks. Be ready for some late nights ahead of you.

When you arrive, wait to be told what to do, and when entering the home, greet everyone with a warm smile and handshake (only if initiated). Follow the directions of your host and sit only when requested; usually, the host does not sit until the guest is sitting.

It is okay to make Mistakes

Your Arab host will do everything to make you feel welcome, comfortable, and happy with their hospitality, even when you make a mistake. If you get something wrong, most likely it is not as bad as you might assume. You will be expected to make a few mistakes and so they will ignore it. You will be forgiven and your host will be extra polite to tell you that you have done something offensive (even if you do not know or mean it); for them, it is rude to point your mistakes out. Therefore, when your host entertains you and provides you with a lot of food, do not make them feel that you are uncomfortable. They enjoy playing the role of the host, their hospitality makes them feel proud; make sure to play into that and show them that you appreciate it and are grateful. It is wise to repeat your thanks more than once. Try to relax and forget about making a mistake, this will help reduce the chance that one will occur.

What to talk about at Home?

To start with, do not bring up business, unless your host does, and never talk about politics or religion. Sharing is part of their culture; people love to show and hear compliments and appreciation. Generosity is taken seriously as part of their honour, therefore, when in their home and you like an item, do not show that you like it, because they will offer it to you. However, if this does happen, it only means that they are being polite, and you should politely refuse it.

When you are ready to leave, your host will ask you to stay, again, as part of their honour, she/he will never end the conversation or suggest to you that it is time for you to leave. When you feel your host is losing interest in the conversations, it is probably time to insist that you should leave. When you leave, they will escort you to the door and, if the relationship is strong, to your car. It is part of their hospitality to make you feel that you are important.

In the West, when you leave someone's house, saying farewell is often brief. In the Arab world, greetings and farewells take a lot longer and, again, this is part of their hospitality. Do your part and participate in the farewells and show that you appreciate it. Always give them the impression that you are honoured to be invited and have the opportunity to connect with them on a personal level. Allow them to feel the pride of being a good host.

Dining
Food

Food is significant in Arab culture. The host will give the best of what they have to their guest as the meal is very important to them. They will offer a varied selection of food and the main meals will always include meat, usually lamb. There is often more food than you can eat. Roasted meats, rice, and freshly made Arab bread are some of the specialities.

Vegetarianism is not always available for the main meal, but the starters are commonly vegetarian. If you are a vegetarian, inform your host and she/he will accommodate your requests. Sometimes, mainly in the GCC, you will be invited to a Bedouin-style meal in the desert. You will sit on the floor around one large dish. You must eat with your right hand. Your host and his relatives will push you to eat and drink, as part of their way of showing hospitality.

The Arabic food is delicious, however, if you do not like it, you must not criticise the food. In some parts of the Arab world, you might offer food like sheep heads. These unusual foods must be taken seriously, you do not have to eat it, but never laugh or be negative.

Pork and Pork Products

In Islam, the consumption of pork and non-Halal animal fats, pork, by-products of pork, and any animals that have not been slaughtered according to Islamic custom is forbidden. Remember, religion is part of everything. Pork or pork products should never be served or even discussed. It is a serious topic to avoid. Your host could be very open-minded and act in a Western way, a large number of them drink alcohol, however, pork is strictly off the menu.

Drinking

In the Arab world, be ready to be caffeinated. You are unlikely to be served Alcohol, therefore, coffee and tea are taking the place of alcohol. In every part of the Arab world, teas and coffee have different variations. For instance, in the Middle East you will be welcomed with the Arabic coffee and in North African countries you will receive delicious green tea.

Arabic coffee is very strong in some parts of the Arab world, such as Jordan and Lebanon. In Saudi coffee is light with a lot of spicy cardamom. Coffee is served in tiny, half-filled thimble cups without handles and poured from a brass jug (Dallah). It is always drunk on arrival and before and after a meal. Remember, if you are meeting in an office, on arrival to the office coffee is used as a welcome but can also be used as a polite request to leave on certain levels (normally with senior government officials). The taste of the coffee may not be to the Westerners taste, but it is important not to show this.

Alcohol

Alcohol is forbidden by Islamic law. However, it is not taken as seriously as pork and the way people deal with it varies from one Arab country to another, mostly due to Westernisation in some part of the Arab world. In some parts, alcohol is illegal to all and you could end up in prison for consuming it. In other countries, alcohol is only illegal for their citizens, and in other parts of the Arab world alcohol is legal but it is only consumed by Westerners and Muslims behind doors. It is necessary to follow the laws on alcohol when in an Arab country. If alcohol is not offered, do not ask for it and do not talk about drinking at business meetings. If you are the host and not sure that your Arab guest drinks alcohol do not offer it. This can offend.

Smoking

In the Arab world be ready to observe a lot of smoking. Even when in Islam, every individual has to pay attention to their health and the health of others around them. However, the majority of Arab smoke, and may even disregard a "no smoking" sign in a workplace, waiting room, or elevators. Smoking is very popular in the Arab world, but even among smokers, it is seen as a bad thing to do. Most Arabs are aware of the dangers of smoking, although many people developed their smoking habit in ignorance of the health dangers involved.

In almost all Arab countries, smoking is seen as inappropriate for women, and it might lead to the ruin of a girl's reputation. However, Narghile/ Shisha smoking, which is more dangerous, by young females is becoming more acceptable than cigarettes in the conservative societies of Arab countries. As a result, Narghile/ Shisha smoking is hugely increased among young Arab females and is more accepted by a large part of the society, including young females. This encourages more and more young females and males to smoke Narghile/ Shisha, which appears to ignore the efficient role of religion and even the conservative Arabic culture.

As a Westerner, when you visit these Narghile/ Shisha places in the Arab world, you may be shocked to see many families gathering around Narghile/ Shisha and many female smokers. Numerous Arabs do not realise that smoking is bad in the presence of others and, in some cases, it is offensive to Westerners. My advice, if you are not so bothered with smoking and have no allergy or health reason, is to ignore it and do not show you are having a bad time.

Gifts

Opening Everything in front of Everyone

Opening Gifts Later by Myself

The giving and receiving of gifts is an important part of social and business life in the Arab world. Gifts reference the sayings of the prophet (the prophet accepted the gift). But what you should gift? for example, Alcohol could be the best gift in Lebanon and the most offensive gift in Saudi. It is advisable to bring a small gift, like honey, chocolates, nuts, or dried fruit. Make sure your gift is always wrapped, and do not be surprised when your host rushes to put it away. It is rude in Arab cultures to open gifts in front of the giver. When you receive a gift, give them your sincere thanks, and do not open it straight away.

Business Socialising in the Arab world

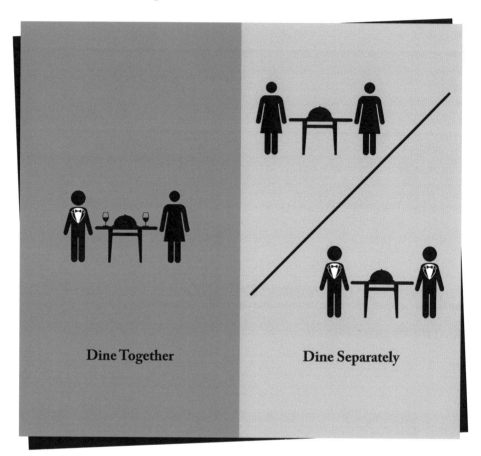

If you are in the Arab world with your spouse, and you are invited to an Arab business event or their home, the invitation is meant for you and not your spouse. The best approach to this is to ask in advance if this is a mixed invitation or just male or female. It is normal in many Arab countries, such as in the GCC, for men and women to dine separately. It is part of the culture that women do not eat with men outside their family. Never ask a man why his wife is not attending a meal or event. If his wife is in attendance, never compliment her look.

Dress to Impress

Be Elegant   Be Elegant and Modest

"Eat what pleases you but wear what pleases others."

This popular saying in the Middle East conveys that image is extremely important.

I recall once, a senior Arab businessperson told me that he did not like the person I introduced him to because when they first met, he could not connect with him. This person was not dressed professionally and did not even comb his hair. He was very laid back in the way he dressed, while the Arab businessperson was all dressed professionally for the meeting.

When in the Arab world, like it or not, you will be judged on how you look. A book is judged by its cover in the Arab world. Arabs believe that you should eat what you want and dress how people want. In the Arab world, your appearance affects how you are perceived and received. Make it your first rule to dress professionally, out of respect. When you are dressed in the right way, the focus will be on the business in hand and your appearance. A professional appearance will impart a message of confidence and authority.

Many Arab societies are concerned with outward appearances as evidence of social status. Good quality clothes reflect a comfortable or powerful position in society. Therefore, it is always important you pay attention to the quality and appearance of the clothes you are wearing if you want to make a lasting impression. Of course, you can dress very similarly to how you usually do, but the important thing is to be smart, stylish, and modest in your dress. Modesty is always a must for both males and females. Although it may vary depending on the country you are in, the idea of modesty in dress applies to almost all Arab societies. In some areas, it is very strict, such as in the Gulf countries because there are stricter traditions. The rest of the Arab world is a little more accepting, but modesty is still the key.

Even in the Gulf region, Bahrain, and the city of Dubai there are many places where you can dress as you like, such as resorts, private beaches, and many other locations. In the Levant, Egypt and North Africa, women are more open with their clothing and you will see and meet many women who dress similar to the West.

Never Dress "Local"

Your Arab counterparts, especially in the Gulf countries, may wear traditional dress. Do not be tempted to don the traditional dress yourself as you may not be taken seriously.

Keep Your Affections to Yourself and Behind Closed Doors

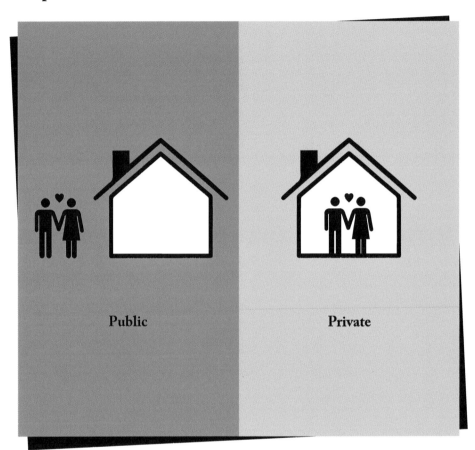

Many Westerns get themselves in trouble in some Arab countries, just by ignoring the culture and its rules. Their tendency for public displays of affection is one of the biggest issues that can get them into trouble. In the West, it is normal for people to kiss or hug each other in public and in front of others, this behaviour is shocking to the very conservative Arab people and culture. Public displays of effect show disrespect to Arab culture and may get you in trouble with the law of the land.

In recent years, there has been media coverage about Westerners getting into trouble in Arab countries. These problems only occur when people ignore or misunderstand culture and regulations.

Homosexuality is also forbidden in the Arab world. If you are in a same-sex relationship, be discreet about it, as it is illegal in most Arab countries. You may see two Arab men greeting each other with kisses or walking together holding hands, this is a way of expressing friendship. It is unlikely for men and women to hold hands or indeed have any form of close physical contact in public.

Any form of a sexual encounter between men and women outside marriage is forbidden in Islam and is illegal in the Arab world. Westerners are indeed treated with more tolerance than Arabs, but Islam forbids sex and homosexual relationships. Publicly, such matters are rarely discussed, and never disregarded. Privately, homosexuality exists among the Arabs but, like other forbidden activity, it is strictly behind closed doors.

Return the Invitation

It is good practice to return the invitation. If you accept an invitation from your Arab counterpart, whether, in the Arab world or your home country, they will expect similar hospitality and generosity in return. Make sure that you meet your Arab counterparts if they are visiting your country, even if they are on holiday. If they are interested in doing business with you, they would love to meet you and keep the relationship going, so make sure you welcome them to the best of your ability and give them the utmost that you have to offer. Pay for all the invitations and act as their guide in the city, even if they know the city. When entertaining, push your guests to have more food and drinks. Go out of your way to impress them. If you are entertaining them out with your colleagues, never try to split the bill in front of them, they will feel impressed. However, always be prepared that your guests might not turn up or they might arrive with other people who you are not aware of.

Personalities & Social Curiosity

The Art of the compliment

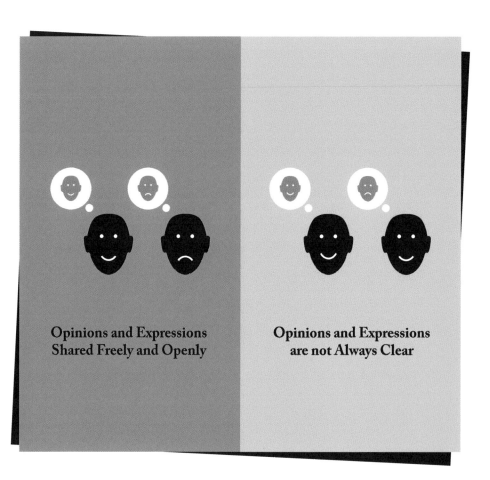

The individuals' behaviour and responsibilities are outlined by the culture and its tradition, which is an important part of Arab culture and has a long history. As such, storytelling and conversations, in general, are important in the Arab world. The stories are oral history, passed down from generation to generation. They tell of everything related to family honour, including generosity, and disputes between families, tribes and countries which can run through generations and cause families to refuse communications between each other. In many cases, tensions pass through generations and people do not talk to each other, without knowing why and or the reasons behind the tension are or why they do not communicate with a certain family. These traditions will eventually affect the way you do business with them.

In Arab culture, everyone is judged by their reputation. It is an obligation and responsibility towards the family, tribe, and community as a whole to have a good reputation. The only way to maintain a good reputation is to follow the traditions of the culture and respect what the older generation have passed on to you and what the society accepts or does not accept. In fact, one's reputation is a matter that is taken seriously. If an individual's reputation is good that will make his family proud and their honour is protected. Whereas, if a family member does something which society and the community disapprove of, then the whole family will feel dishonour and be subjected to gossip and exaggerated stories which can be repeated and fabricated and last for many generations to come.

Privacy

Relax, you are in the Arab world and your privacy is something you must allow to be invaded.

When you are in the Arab world, you will find that Arabs are very curious people and they will ask you many personal questions to befriend you and do business with you. You also can do the same to them, but be very careful, choose your subject correctly and ask the right questions. For example, in some cases, asking for a female member of the family can be inappropriate. Even if you have dined with your business counterpart and his wife before, you cannot ask about her as he might feel uncomfortable to talk about her in front of other family members or friends in his country. Follow your counterparts lead in what is appropriate to make sure that yours and their honour is not insulted.

Compliments

Compliments are an art in the Arab world. People enjoy hearing them and also enjoy giving them. They say nice things about other people's houses, children, cars, and new things that they have bought. All of these are signs of respect and honour toward the receiver.

You can use compliments as an important way to win business and make new friends. Compliments are a way of life for Arabs, they play a big part in encouraging people's confidence and they are a positive social practice which brings people together and establishes relationships.

Arabs will do anything to avoid saying something which you might not like to hear; some might just fabricate something that they believe is the answer you wish to hear, such as saying something suitable for the occasion.

Words are Powerful

Remember, words in the Arab world travel fast and it can cause good and bad things, especially in business. When speaking with Arabs, remember that they believe that words have power. Therefore, blessings are very important to Arabs and are used in their conversations and greetings to maintain the occurrence of good things happening and cancel bad ones. They will also use euphemisms when discussing the plight of others. For instance, say a mutual acquaintance is ill and near death. Should you inquire about recent news they will likely respond, "he is well, but a little tired"?

Arabs, like most of the Mediterranean region, believe in the evil eye, "Ayn Al-hasud" in Arabic. They do not talk about pleasantries, because they believe negative words make a negative outcome.

When you admire someone's car, office, animal, or anything they own, they believe your blank admiration will bring a malicious force that might cause harm and damage to the thing that you admired. Arabs believe that they can deflect the eye of envy by using certain religious charms and the name of God. For example, if you meet an Arab family and see their child and the child is beautiful or has nice eyes or hair, you should say "Masha'Allah" "What God Wills." how beautiful, God keeps them safe." Always add good wishes and involve God "may God bless him." This religious charm is believed to bring protection. Additional phrases from the Quran are also thought to help.

The colour blue is also used to protect children and properties. Charms made from blue glass beads with an eye are used to keep evil away, because blue is the colour of the eye of envy. In the Arab world, Arab Christians also believe in the evil eye, "Ayn Al-hasud" and the use of blue beads or blue glass to ward off the eye of envy.

Blue beads or religious signs are used in cars and house doors to help keep evil away. This is part of Arab culture, even for those who are not religious. It is often also used on social media accounts as protection from bad attention from others.

In an Arab business, information from a friend or a relative is regarded as the truth and will hold great value, as such, rumours in the region will travel fast and may cause damage. When doing business in the Arab world, it is very important to pay great attention to the words that you use. You may even be able to use words for your advantage. For example, when Arabs go to buy something, they might say to shop workers "I am here because my cousin told me about your shop." The intention is to say what the counterpart wants to hear and also to push them to provide you with the best service. In Business, words can also indicate a lot about your personality and can play a huge part in first impressions.

When you do business with the Arabs and negotiate with them, the words you use are part of your success and can be essential to closing a deal. They may put you in a better position when negotiations start so that you have more possibilities for further business and a long-term partnership.

The Difference between a Western "No" and an Arab "No"

One of the main goals for Arabs, socially, is to express their knowledge and power. The host at a multimillion-dollar corporate company, or a corner shop staff, will both avoid saying "No" or other phrases that use a directly negative outcome. In Western culture, the use of the word "No" to refuse or deny something is commonly used and is not considered rude. Whereas, in the Arab world it is rude and considered a very harsh way to deal with people. Even Admitting, "I don't know" is distasteful to an Arab.

This is one of the reasons why Arabs are known to speak using vague terms, tell diversion stories, use words with double meanings, and answer a question with another question, when they do not want to answer or to give an answer might offend and make them lose face. It can be annoying that Arabs' tend to say "yes" when they mean "no".

In the Arab world, replying "no" to a question is almost rude, or unkind, they might think that you are being unhelpful, which would lead to a loss of face. For example, an Arab might say yes to an invitation because he does not want to hurt your feelings, but he knows that he cannot make it. In the West, if someone did not want to go then they would decline the invitation, with or without an excuse. Or, they will say "I'll try to make it but don't count on me." What seems like a firm declaration to Westerns may seem weak or doubtful to Arabs, and statements which seem to Arabs to be simple statements of fact may seem to be extreme to Westerns.

If an Arab says yes to your request, this does not necessarily mean that they are certain that the action will be carried out. Following their etiquette, means that their response to your request must be positive. Yet, the result may be another thing; even if they have to deal with its consonances later on.

Delivering Bad News

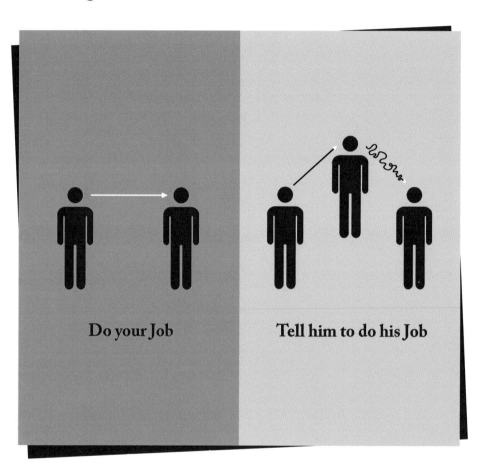

For a culture like the Arab world, feelings are important, that is why breaking bad news to anyone is always not an easy thing to do. For example, in the Arab world, it is very common for a doctor not to tell a sick person what is exactly wrong with them, unlike in the West.

Arabs, in general, believe they should try to avoid being the person delivering bad news. Therefore, sometimes, there will be no response if the response is negative. In many cases in the Arab world, you will experience a delay in response which is the result of trying to save face by not delivering the bad news to you. They may instead ask someone else to deliver it to you.

In business, feedback must include saving face to preserve personal honour and dignity. If bad news is delivered personally it will be done indirectly or by just giving some signs. It will never be given directly, which in some cases makes it difficult to know what the news is.

Arab Names; How Should I Address People?

Like everything else in Arab culture, names are very important to the Arab people. Names tell someone if they know the person and where they are from, such as the city or village just through the family name, which classifies the person in terms of lineage, an individual's tribe, and family status. Also, many Arabic names have a meaning, so it is very helpful to know the name of a person. Arabs, still write their names in the passport with first, second, third and family names and they recite the names of great grandfathers back many generations.

When you are introduced to someone it is important to remember their name and focus on it. Use the old mythology of repeating it in your head, use it when you talk to him/her. Arabic names are not easy to remember and to say correctly, but if you use it straight after they say it, your chances of getting right are much bigger. Of course, some of the names are very difficult to pronounce, and they do not expect you to pronounce it correctly, but it is wise to read the name in English before you meet the person to avoid the embarrassment of pronouncing the name very badly. How would you feel if someone kept pronouncing your name badly?.

Never use the name without the titles unless you are invited by the individual to do so. Remember, when with high profile people, even if they allow you to call them by the first name, never do it in the presence of their staff or other guests, it is your way of showing respect, do it privately, and never in business meetings or during formal negotiations. You must familiarise yourself with the proper use of titles. It is not complicated and is part of the politeness you are required to use. Such as using the title Your Highness for members of the royal family and Excellency for government ministers or high-ranking officials.

Arabs can also be very casual with names when doing business and generally when addressing people. They do this by addressing people as Mr / Mrs followed by their first name. For a Westerner, this can be a surprise to be addressed in this way, but it is their way of showing respect. For example, Mrs Mary Robinson will be called Mrs Mary and Mr John Smith will be called Mr John. This also works with different titles, such as Professor Marry and Dr John.

When you address a male, but you do not know their title you should always say Mr Adam or Sayyid Adam or Ustaz Adam for Adam. If you are addressing a woman, never address an Arab woman without a title: Sayyidah Safaa (Madam Safaa) would be well received.

It is also very wise to check the meaning of your name in the Arabic language; you will be surprised that your name might have a very rude meaning in their language. This could cause embarrassment to you and them; do not be surprised if it puts people off doing business and you end up losing the contract.

TRUST ME,
I'M

عربي

Social Media in The Arab World

If we can't Solve it via Email, let's use WhatsApp

Social media and your online presence, like anything else in the Arab world, is different than in the West. You have to apply the cultural sensitivities and conservative culture of the Arab world to your communications as it will play a big part for winning customers and maybe a religious or cultural blunder that might lose a contract. A business will avoid a deal with any brands that might insult the culture or religion. For example, social media accounts must show modesty and must not make fun of any respected figures from the past or the present. In some parts of the Arab world, females are very cautious whom they befriend on social media and about what pictures they share. It is very common that a lot of people, mainly females, do not use their real names.

Westerners doing business with Arabs you should be aware of these differences and understand their online behaviours. People in the Arab world are young, they are the right market for brands and big social media companies. In general, Arabs are always online and are very active users of social media; they are considered one of the highest social media users in the world. More than half of the population has access to the internet and, as a result, social media is changing the way Arabs live. "Consumers in the Middle East and North Africa (Mena) are among the most active users of social media platforms. The region's large youth population and high mobile penetration rate have made it the ideal market for companies like Instagram and Snapchat, but it is Facebook that remains the most dominant platform for the Middle East with more than 180 million users, up from 56 million just five years ago." *(Hamid, T, 2019).*

Using Social Media for Businesses

Social media in the Arab world has increased since the introduction of Facebook and Twitter in the region. A large number of Arabs communicate in English. Social media, marketing and word of mouth are essential. They are being targeted by big brands through social media. You need to understand how communication and marketing are changing.

This varies within the Arab world, for example, in the GCC Snapchat and Instagram are hugely popular, whereas Facebook is no longer popular. It does, however, remain the most dominant platform in Egypt. What is interesting about Facebook in the GCC countries, is huge for the foreigners, especially the Asians (India, Pakistan, Bangladesh, Philippines) and lower among the nationals.

Twitter is also widely used and is very important in Saudi, and Snapchat is the real success story in the GCC, mainly for luxury brands and big business. Snapchat is the most popular platform in the conservative GCC countries because messages and posts disappear after 24 hours and the user will be notified if someone takes a screenshot of their conversation. Privacy is the main attraction for the users, both males and females.

As with Snapchat, Instagram is also popular for Arab females and both big and small brands. A lot of businesses use both platforms, tailoring them for the Arab market, and, very importantly, respecting the cultural aspect of the Arab World.

In recent years, there has been a huge Chinese presence in the Arab world large investments have been made in many parts of the Arab world by Chinese companies and the Chinese government and the large increase of Chinese students and tourists. As a result, there is a huge presence of Chinese technology in the region, including the social media platform Tik Tok, which has made a big and fast mark on the Arab world. This is a brilliant and current example for Western businesses and companies and the competition in which they face.

When in the Arab World Download WhatsApp

Make sure you have WhatsApp when you work with the Arabs, they prefer to use it to send documents as they see it as more secure, faster, and easier than other options. WhatsApp remains the most popular social media platform in the region.

The use of WhatsApp by small businesses and Instagram private accounts mainly by women demonstrate the use of closed, and sometimes gendered, groups in social media and shows how they are adjusting the use of social media to meet their culture.

Be Careful

With the popularity of social media in the Arab world, it is important to remember cyber-security laws are very tight. Therefore, users are cautious with what they say online. A large number of users support their government's cyber-security regulations and want them to block sites and material that do not keep them and their children safe. They also support block sites and material which criticise religion or historical figures.

TRUST ME,
I'M
عربي

How to do Business with the Arabs

The Unwritten Rules

Let's do Business   Let's Talk

The Arab world is one of the most promising and misunderstood markets in the world. Despite a large part of the region suffering from poverty and economic inequality, it still offers great opportunities for business and jobs outside the oil industry. The Arab world benefits from one of the highest GDP/capita rates in the world and has a young population and a growing labour force industry.

Often Westerners approach business in the Arab world with the stereotype that the 'Arab' way of doing business is unprofessional, it is always impossible to know what they want, and it is better to avoid the business dealing with them.

In the past decade, the Arab world has undergone many social, political, and even religious transitions. Doing business in the Arab region is associated with a certain set of business and cultural practices that cannot be ignored. Whether you are in Morocco in Africa or Saudi Arabia in Asia, you have to be aware of the cultural differences between yourself and your new business partners. Understanding how Arabs think, act, and do business is part of a successful business with the Arabs. You must learn the Arab way of doing business. If you do not, you will lose out on important opportunities to grow your business.

In the last few decades, Western media has reported on Arab culture, people, and the region as a whole. Many of these reports are based on assumptions. These biased reports have increased Arab frustration at times with the West. As someone looking to do business with the Arabs, it is your job to understand the rich traditions of Arab religion and culture and to show your counterparts that you are not influenced by what the media or any other stereotypes in the West might present. Having this approach and awareness will help you to establish a very trusting relationship and a long-term business with them. By understanding your Arab counterpart's, you will be successful in the personal relationship which is the main step towards securing your professional goals.

In the Arab world, you will be faced by a market which will vary from country to country, and even from one situation to another. Each Arab country has its cultural nuances and subtle differences that affect how the business market operates. Assuming that you can use the same approach in every country will cause you difficulties. It is therefore important to do your research carefully and work with the right people and be culturally prepared or you risk the chance of offending those you wish to impress. However, the region can offer you unique opportunities to grow your business if you are prepared to decipher the Arab business etiquette.

Where to Begin

Do not start doing business without a strategy! It is that simple. For your business and products to succeed in the region, first it has to appeal to the local culture and religion.

Successful businesses will adopt an international image and use it to make their Arab customers and business partners pleased with what they offer. Indeed, the Arab world can be different from the West, and you have to develop a tailored approach and understand the culture to understand the market.

If it is your first time in the Arab world, you will greatly benefit from researching and learning about the country you are visiting and about Arabic history and culture. This will help you when it comes to building the relationship with the ones you are investing to do business with, for instance, by showing your knowledge of Arabic history, you will impress, thus aiding your business relationship. If you begin business proceedings without giving yourself enough time to understand, you will run into difficulties very quickly. As you will have realised whilst reading this book, a business deal can be easily and quickly ruined through misunderstandings and wrong approaches.

Business is Personal

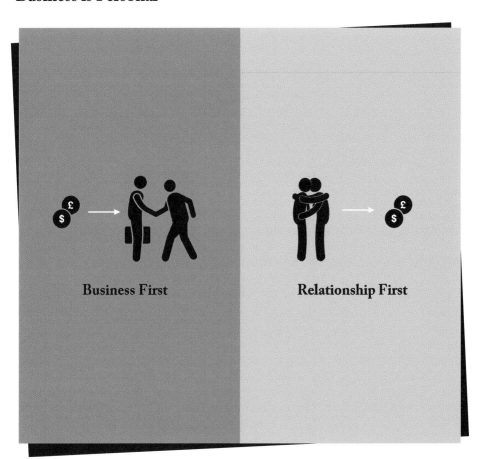

For the Arabs, every business arrangement is an opportunity to develop a real personal relationship which will lead to more business in the future. For a successful business deal, it is important to let your counterpart know that you wish for a long relationship and not just a one-off contract.

In order to work successfully in the region, take the time to make friends. By having trusted friends in the Arab world, business will become easier and the normal rules of business will be broken to accommodate you. Take your time to get to know your Arab partners, what interests them and what is important to them outside their business. However, if you are unwilling to change your approach and behaviour, you will find that doors will close.

Generally, Westerners separate their personal lives from business so that business is not influenced by personal preferences, such as family and friends. Conversely, Arab businesses are centred around the family and relationships. Arabs respect the Western business style, however, interpret it as a very cold way to work. The concepts of personal relationships, family ties, trust and honour, and hospitality are all part of Arab business deals. Therefore, your business relationships will be built on mutual friendship and trust. A reliable relationship will be valued over profit.

In short, Arabs place the personal relationship before anything else and if they trust you and you manage to gain confidence, then they will be comfortable to start doing business with you.

Appointments & Meetings

"Wasta" Not What You Know but Who You Know

One of the biggest challenges facing newcomers to the Arab world is gaining a chance to get a foot in the door and meet the right people. There are two ways to do this, you can do the work and contact companies and organisations in the Arab world directly or you can find a "Wasta". In the Arab World, you need to build your own "Wasta". Which refers to using one's connections and/or influence to get things done, including government transactions. It is the westerner's way of saying "I'll scratch your back if you'll scratch mine" which includes the cultural differences and the favours between the Arabs and Westerners.

In the Arab world, everyone has a "Wasta". It is an essential way to access contacts outside the formal channels. The "Wasta" will refer you to a network of influential people which will benefit your business and achieve both small and large goals. For instance, if you need your broadband connected straightaway or waiving a traffic fine just call your "Wasta", or if you want to meet with the Prime Minister, call your "Wasta". Without it, not much will be achieved. Some people call it the Arab Vitamin "W" because it is behind small and large business transactions in the Arab world. "Wasta" is as simple as knowing someone who knows someone or by paying or hiring someone for their contacts. When hired, a "Wasta" will not do any work but they will open doors.

Connection or Corruption

By using their influence to do a favour for someone, the person doing the "Wasta" gets the honour and the one receiving the "Wasta" will have debts which he has to repay in the future. It is a key part of Arab culture and business. Again, as everything is personal in the Arab world "Wasta" is part of family obligations which people feel no shame being a part of. For example, when an Arab has a problem, or needs something outside the official channels, the first thing they will do is look for a friend or relative in the right place to help.

This can take many shapes; I have seen many big Western companies hiring the son or relative of a very high official dignitary to work for them. In return, the father guarantees the opening of many locked doors.

However, do not take this information as a green light to behave this way, you have to be careful. Sometimes, "Wasta" can lead to liability under anti-corruption law in some Arab countries, and, if you do not understand the key backgrounds you could easily run into trouble with the law. You are there to do business and make money, you do not want to end up in court. In some Arab markets, even a simple mistake, such as bouncing a cheque, can get you into a lot of trouble. Therefore, make sure that you are aware of the relevant penalties for financial misdemeanours so that you can avoid them.

Arranging Initial Meetings

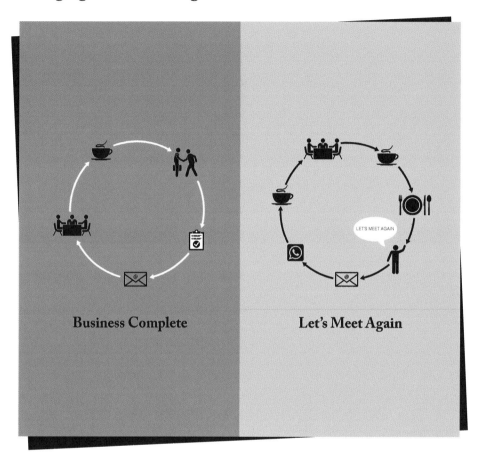

Business Complete

Let's Meet Again

Now it is time to arrange the appointment. Take a deep breath, this process can be frustrating in some parts of the Arab world as arrangements will change a lot.

It is normal for a meeting to take several months to arrange and, in some cases, it may never take place. Also, it may be that you call and say I am in town and asked to come straight away. If you do not have other people to contact and your counterpart is unavailable, try to reschedule the meeting with a deputy or personal assistant.

Getting Appointments and Meeting People

In the West, you can arrange a meeting with someone's secretary who will usually have access to their boss's diary. In the Arab world, your appointments must be made with the individual concerned. The secretary will not have access to the boss's diary and, even if she/ he has access, they will not have the authority to make an appointment. You will, therefore, benefit from making appointments before your travel. But remember, the further in advance an appointment is made, the less likely it will occur.

The Value of the Personal Visits

Like any other market, personal visits are important to start business development. In the Arab world, it expected that you visit on many occasions, more than you would visit counterparts elsewhere. Always give the impression that you are ready to visit whenever it is needed. Do not expect deals to be completed in one visit to the region.

Indeed, in the Arab world, you must meet your business counterpart to do business. Emails and phone calls will not be enough to start a deal or for business success; Arabs are famous for not replying to emails. To make an appointment to meet with a new partner, pick up the phone, talking to them to arrange the meeting is a good way to start. A visit should follow this so that you can develop a business relationship face to face. For your first visit to the Arab world, make sure that you have a programme full of appointments so that you meet many people and increase your chance of a successful outcome. When organised multiple meetings, ensure that there is a considerable time between each meeting to accommodate delays. In the Arab world, if you are serious about long-term success in the region, you must invest time. Contracts will not succeed, and business will not grow through limited trips to the Arab world. Ensure regular trips, always meet your targets, and slowly build trust and friendships.

One thing to remember, finding the location of a meeting is not always straightforward, since street names and building numbers are not well marked and many have similar names.

The Concept of Time

I'm Always on Time   "Inshaalah"

Arabs measured time in days, by the sunrise and sunset, rather than time in minutes. A one o'clock meeting may not start until three o'clock or may be cancelled. For example, you may be asked to meet after the dawn prayer tomorrow' or after sunset or in the evening, such imprecise times makes it no wonder that appointments are missed! Meetings should not be made too far in advance as changes in personal circumstances may impact the appointment. Once an appointment has been made, it is wise to confirm it verbally with the person you will meet a few days beforehand.

Arabs do not see the point of keeping busy so as not to waste time and would never complain that they are "too busy" to something important to them. Even in workplaces time is very relaxed. There are no strict rules about breaks, and there are frequent social interactions with visitors.

However, while in most cases business moves slowly in the Arab world, many things are changing and many of the young generations aim to make money fast. Therefore, things can move faster than you expect, and, in some cases, the Arabs may want your deals to finalise much quicker than you have planned and they put you under pressure.

"Ma'alesh", "Bukra" and "Inshaalah"

Relax you are in the Arab world, be patient and take your time and learn the three words: Ma'alesh, "Inshaallah" and Bukra

Three words are important for you to remember to understand the differences between Arabs and Westerns:

"Ma'alesh" means "it's Okay." You will hear this when something which should have happened but did not, or something was carried out in a way you are not happy with, or if you are not happy with someone who is not doing their job. In instances like these, you will be told Ma'alesh from the people around you.

"Bukra" means "tomorrow" in Arabic. However, this does not always mean the following day. It is most often used to mean the future. For your Arab counterparts, they believe that only God knows the future, so take it easy. You might face a problem that you want to solve urgently, and you have been promised that it will be dealt with tomorrow, but when tomorrow comes nothing happens. Perhaps, you are waiting for some important paperwork and when you ask, a promise is made that it will be " Bukra" "tomorrow". It is also good to know Ba'ad Bukra which means "after tomorrow" and is often used to mean sometime soon, perhaps in a few weeks.

"Inshaallah", It is actually a phrase and not one word, put together for easier pronunciation. You will hear repeatedly in conversations between Arabs. It means "God willing.". "Inshaallah" embodies the Arab philosophy of fatalism. It is a religious expression for God willing in the future and is supposed to be used to say yes. However, in business, it is most likely used as a no. Unfortunately, this religious word is often used outside its context, and far away from the religious meaning.

Indeed, "Inshaallah" can mean many different things. In business, you should use it as a promise, it could also mean 'I hope so', or 'I will try my best'. The word is not used as an excuse for laziness as many Westerners believe.

"Inshaallah"

The word became well-known in the west after the Gulf War. More recently, it was used during the first US presidential debate of the 2020 campaign, when former vice president Joe Biden pushed his rival President Donald Trump to release his tax returns. Mr Trump replied that he would release his records "when they were ready." Mr Biden replied, "when? Inshallah," using the Arabic word for God willing. While the term is often used sincerely, colloquially it can also be used to indicate something unlikely to happen. It literally means "God willing," but it is often used to mean, "Yeah, this is never going to happen."

"It is also important to point out that lately many Arab countries have adopted a different business style and time is respected, not all business services run like this and there is an increasing move towards the punctuality of appointments."

Your First meeting is not a Business Meeting

The first meeting will be a general meeting. It will not cover what you are there for and will instead contain a lot of irrelevant talk like about your trip, such as, if you have seen the city and what you think of it. This meeting is all about the process of getting to know each other. You must relax, smile, and listen. They will not talk about business and you should not bring it up. The process of establishing a business relationship takes time, so if you are thinking a couple of days with back to back meetings will work, think again. It is important to invest the time to develop a relationship and succeed in your business aims.

Always plan for several meetings rather than putting all your eggs in one basket. If all aims are met on the first meeting then this is great, and you can go back home relax and you are on your way to success. However, if you are an employee, and you need more time for this, ensure that your boss is aware that you might need more time than planned.

It is normal to be asked to wait when you visit people. However, do not wait too long, as this might send the wrong message. Never look bored. If it is the first meeting, they will watch you all the time and ensure you are someone they can trust. The meeting will be long and can run for hours. At the early stages of building a trusting relationship you should expect meetings with the senior and decision-makers to be short; always be ready to impress them with your personality.

Meetings outside the office environment are common. If this opportunity is presented to you, take it; business will be discussed in a more relaxed way and results are usually better. Whenever you have the chance to visit your Arab partners, ensure that you do, even if you do not have any business to discuss with them. Social meetings are common in the Arab world and, sometimes, Arabs will feel there is no relationship if you only visit them for business or when you need something.

The Second Meeting

In the second meeting, the business might be discussed in some detail. However, if you are still in the early stages of your business relationship, so the meeting will also be used to get to know you, establish facts about your business, and assess if you are the right business partner. Once this is established, then the business will begin. It remains, however, dependant on how your counterpart feels, so be ready for all scenarios. One important rule to follow when you meet with the Arabs, whether your meeting was a success or a failure, is to always follow the meeting with a call. This is important to fix any misunderstanding or confirm understanding.

Arriving at the Meeting

A British businesswoman from the banking industry was visiting Qatar where she was to meet an influential and wealthy Qatari lady about a private banking matter. She had made the appointment more than a month before and confirmed it on the phone with her office one day before the meeting. When she turned up, she had to wait for more than an hour before she agreed to see her. By that time, she was frustrated and angry and forgot that she should be polite and nice. She showed her frustration and complained that she has another meeting to go to and she will have to make the meeting quick. The meeting was quick, but also was not a success and the Bank lost a very important client.

Arabs admire the punctuality of Westerners. When they want to talk about an accurate time, they say it will be "Mow'aad Englizey" 'English Timing'. ; However, it is normal for your partner to be late or to change the meeting at short notice. It is important that you take this in your stride and do not show that you are frustrated. Arabs feel that punctuality is very important, but they do not always practice it. It is important, though, that you are not late. If you are running late do not panic as a polite excuse will be accepted.

In the Arab world, meetings usually will not have an exact end time. If you are asked to change the time of a meeting, do so, they will appreciate your flexibility and patience. This will help you win their respect once you show that you have recognised your understanding and appreciate how their culture works.

If your host is late, take it easy. This can be due to a more important visitor, or to personal or family matters which for Arabs are more important than business. They might say 'My father called me, and I have to go and see him'. Time is a major area of culture clash between the Arabs and Westerns; being flexible with timing usually works to your advantage.

Entering the Meeting

When entering the meeting, instead of saying "hello" it is advised that you use the traditional Islamic greeting "Assalamow Aleikum," which translates to "May peace be upon you". By using this icebreaker, your meeting might have the right start. Try to greet the most senior person first when you enter (if happen to know who he/she is). In order to find out who is who, it is important to treat any introductions in meetings with great respect. Follow your host's direction in the discussion during a meeting.

In general, start with a handshake, these may take longer than you are used to in the West. Wait for the other person to withdraw their hand before you do so. If you are shaking hands with an Arab woman, wait for her to offer her hand. As part of the conservative culture, she might not shake hands at all. If you are a Western businesswoman, you should do the same. Wait for the male to offer his hand for the handshake and be prepared that an Arab man might shake hands with your colleague or husband/partner but not with you. Remain standing until you are invited to sit down and remember that you should also stand when a senior person enters or leaves the room. Maintain eye to eye contact with your counterpart even if you are talking through a translator.

Put your watch on your pocket as checking your watch is considered rude and demonstrates that you do not take them seriously and you have more important things to attend to. If you are important, and the relationship has already developed, or is developing well then punctual timekeeping is more likely to happen. In the early stages of relationship building, the people who have a better relationship will have priority.

Ensure that you are not impatient since this will be interpreted badly. If you have to leave, you should have a very good excuse such as a flight and show them how sorry you are.

At the Meeting: The Chit Chat

"Right, let's get to business."

The director of a big European company is expanding to Abu Dhabi. He has just arrived in the country and is meeting with a senior decision-maker of the company with whom he wants to work with. After greeting him and exchanging a few words for a couple of minutes he tried to change the topic of conversation to business. He said to his Arab counterpart, "Right, let's get to business." Unfortunately, his host felt that he was wasting his time and that the man did not have time for him. The warm welcome turned to a cold and short conversation.

If the European director had some knowledge about the Arab way of doing business, he would prepare himself to be aware of the time spent before business.

As you are used to doing business in the West, a quick comment about the weather that day is usually all that is needed before the meeting moves onto discussing the agenda. This does not work in the Arab world, if you are not ready to spend time talking about irrelevant topics and you want to jump straight to business, then you will be perceived as a rude businessperson. Arabs love the chit chat; this is how they do business. When the meeting begins allow your counterpart to change the conversation to business, do not do this yourself.

Lack of Privacy

Privacy   Lack of Privacy

A Westerner in an important business meeting with a senior government official in Morocco, he is shocked that the door was not closed, and people interrupted even though he was meeting with a very senior official. The Westerner felt that the meeting was not taken seriously by the Moroccan officials and they might not be as important as he thought before.

In the Arab world, everybody has time for everybody else, for business, friends, and conversation. People will enter the room, phone calls will be answered, and messages will be replied to. This is not conserved to be rude. When you are at a meeting in the Arab world, it is normal for you to find other people in the room at the same time. Or, maybe while you are there other people enter the room, without an appointment, for a chat or business. If this happens you do not have to leave but try to take a lead from your host. Do not be surprised or take it personally, for Arabs, it is courtesy.

In the Arab culture, it is rude to tell someone that they need to leave, even if someone else is waiting and if they are available and at the same time, it is rude to make you wait. So, to avoid rudeness to both people, the solution is to have you both meetings at the same time. Be prepared for your host to start talking business in their presence. It is not an ideal situation, but it is normal. Do not be put off by this, learn to join in the conversation and get to know these guests as they might be important for you in the future. Allow this to happen, take a deep breath, smile, and relax.

Remember, you are being judged for how patient you are and if you are the right business partner. My advice, when your meeting is interrupted, is to use this time to prepare your thoughts and ideas again, perhaps also look around the office and find something to compliment your host for. The right time and opportunity to discuss your business will present itself to you, you need to know when and how to use it.

The Agenda

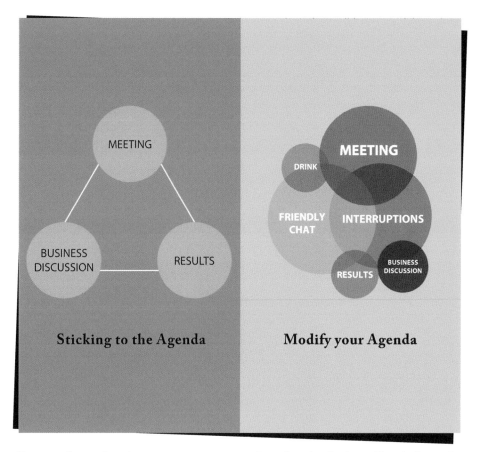

Now, you know that the way meetings are conducted in the Arab world is different from what you are used to in the West. To aid you further, you need to know that the agenda of the meeting is not important, and the discussion could vary greatly and change without linear direction. This is why the preliminary meeting should be a light one; they will not appreciate it if you try to do a lot of work at the meeting. Be yourself and engage with the conversation. Through this, you will learn more about each other which will aid your counterpart in deciding why they should work with you. Talk about yourself, they will appreciate it, talk about your travels and what you do. Listen to their stories and tell your own stories, stories about your home, your experiences in other countries, your health, business, art, culture, sport, and your family. If your Arab partner is in a hurry, they will discuss the business straightway, if not, forget that you are there for the business meeting until they bring it up. Small talk is not a waste of time, it is important to establish trust and warmth before the business begins.

Agenda action points may be raised in the last few minutes whilst you are getting ready to leave.

Also, remember when you are meeting high senior people, agendas with senior officials are important. However not everything on the agenda will be discussed, and, as with other meetings, not everything you will talk about will be on the agenda, always be ready for surprises.

The Personal Questions

In the Arab, world many people are now learning to respect the Western idea of privacy, but you will still come across people who will be very direct with their questioning. Be expected to answer questions about family and lifestyle; this is how they show their interest in you. Prepare yourself for very personal questions, such as asking how old you are, if you are divorced, what salary you earn, if you married, or if you have children. You should also ask questions; take the lead from them but always try to avoid the topics of politics, religion, stereotypes, illness, accidents, death, bad luck of any kind, or anything that could cause embarrassment. When the questions are too personal and if you feel uncomfortable answering, then answer differently. Such as, I love my job and the salary is worth a lot to me, or if they ask how old you are, could say, I am young at heart and feel 18. In all cases, you are not obliged to answer them. However, be polite by redirecting the question.

Unsafe Topics

Politics

I personally lost contact because I have made my political view clear to someone who I thought was a close friend. However, once I said something about his government which he did not like, he stopped talking to me since.

If you are asked a political question, you can try to give an upbeat yet neutral answer and navigate the conversation towards a new subject. Arabs enjoy talking about politics, but they will not bring it up directly and not in the first meeting. If politics is brought up, you could say that you are not aware of the subject. This would be a good time to ask them to teach you more about the subject. Arabs like to talk about politics as if they are experts. It is important that you listen to them and do not tell them your honest opinion. Always remember that you are there to do business, not to win a political argument. This leads us to an important point, never criticise the Arab governments or their Royal Family. This is punishable with prison and can lead to serious consequences. It may also offend your Arab counterparts who will think you rude and disrespectful, resulting in you losing the contract. So, make sure you do not rush to give your opinion on the local issues. For example, in the GCC countries, when speaking about the area, you might say the Persian Gulf which can cause a big problem for the local Arabs who believe that it is called the Arab Gulf. Moreover, never use the phrase "You Arabs" which is demeaning and rude.

Religion

The same applies to religion. Even two members of the same religion can have differing views, which can easily risk a misunderstanding. Religion can be a touchy subject to Arabs, so any words can cause irreversible damage, even if it was accidental. This is why it is sensible to avoid the topic of religion altogether and never criticise Islam or comment of the Prophet Muhammad. Show great respect to religious sensitivities at all times, if you do not, your job or contract will be in danger. You have no way of knowing when and how you might offend another individual when discussion topics about religion evolve, particularly today. Keep your opinions to yourself, it does not matter what you believe.

Good topics for Conversation

There are some topics that you will never go wrong with. These include talking about travel, and the weather. Family is always a good topic to talk about. You could ask about their health, how many children they have, or where they studied or are about to study; although never ask specific questions about their wife, daughter, or female family members. Sport is also a brilliant topic to discuss. Arabs love sports, especially football, hunting and horse and camel racing. It may help you to talk about how impressed you are with the country's landmarks, cuisine, culture, and, as your relationship develops, you may well find that he or she will be happy to discuss local matters freely. Most important, however, is that you listen. There is nothing more important or interesting to most Arab people than themselves. Let them talk about themselves and listen, listen, and listen some more. If you do so, that person will likely leave the conversation feeling as though you were an extremely engaging individual and will remember the encounter as a positive experience.

Use your Manners

Arabs like humour. Laugh at their silly jokes but avoid sarcasm. They can be very funny people and enjoy a good joke, however, avoid jokes which do not translate well. It is sensible to avoid bad language. Arabs do not find jokes about their country, the Arab world, religion, government, culture, leaders, or their food funny. Do not joke about these things. What is viewed as funny and engaging by a Western could be insulting to Arabs, do not risk this. It is also wise not to make fun of yourself or others, this can be interpreted as rude and insulting.

The Aftermath of the Meeting

No Tit-for-Tat Approach

If you want a successful business, follow-up and drive the process yourself.

Many Western companies take the hospitality, kindness, and politeness of their Arab counterparts at meetings as signs of success. On many occasions, I have heard people say that they had a great visit, good meeting, that their counterparts liked them and loved their products, but then they did not hear from their Arabs partners after that, despite calling and emailing. 'I followed up and called more than ten times and sent several emails with no response' - you might experience this, but it is important to keep trying. Today, the advancement of technology means that an email can be sent instantaneously, but it is essential that you always follow-up by phone. It is even better if you can visit them. If you do email, you may not receive a quick response or no response at all. Face to face contact is the most important way of communicating, with email contact being the least. Of course, this is changing and depends on the industry and the country you work with.

What I am saying here is that, while it is true that you had a good meeting and they loved your products, your pitch was one of many from someone they did not know. Their priority is to establish a business relationship, that is why it is essential to follow up and concentrate on building that relationship. This process must continue after all meetings, particularly when dealing with the high net worth Arabs who are less likely to need the deals much as you do. Make follow up calls up to ten times, even if these are to ask how the person is, without bringing up the business or the subject you planned to discuss. This is important to make them feel that you are interested in them and in building the relationship.

When you call them, and it is to discuss business, keep your phone calls brief and focus on the important issues. Your contact will have many things to do and he probably will not take any notes. He may also be dealing with many calls like yours, that is why, even when they do not reply to your emails, it is wise to follow up your phone call with an e-mail or if the relationship is established with a text message or a WhatsApp, to state what you discussed or just say thank you.

Do not call them on Friday and during Ramadan, they will not answer, although they might call you at 7 am on Sunday and expect you to answer.

Listening and Presentation

Presentations

Arabs and Westerners have completely different speech styles. In the West people in business tend to be brief and to the point, whereas for the Arabs this seems rushed and not the right approach to work with people.

Arabs also elaborate on subjects which are not relevant. If they are rushed into a business, they will say whatever the other person wants to hear. If you are trying to make them confirm a decision, they may say "Inshaallah Bukrah".

Arabs are interested in what they can understand fast without any complications. They are very impatient listeners and, sometimes when they nod or smile during presentations, it does not mean they understand you or they are agreeing with what you are presenting. They do so to be polite.

When presenting your business in any form, talking or on screen, make sure that your presentation is designed carefully. A small thing like an inappropriate image or a word can cause an offence and damage to your business. Keep in mind that Arabs like very well organised and stylish presentations, both on-screen and in the materials you hand out. Ensure it does not include too much information and technicality; unless it is for a specific sector and it is needed.

If you are a shy and quiet speaker, you may lose their attention straight away. This is why it is always useful to have an employee who is good at talking and presenting. Never send a junior or a young member of your team to deal with the top people, it has to be one of the senior partners.

Your English

When dealing with people from different cultures, no matter how smart, qualified, and experienced they are in their business, the way of doing business and terms and expression used in their languages are different. This means that almost half of what you are saying may be misconstrued, so they will miss some important information which could be a key factor to your business, and it will open the door for potential misunderstandings and disagreement. The little things that you think they know, they might not know it, so never assume that they will understand what you mean. A plain translation of the phrase will not help them or you. Any small details that they do not understand might lead to essential information being missed and the whole pitch will be a waste of time.

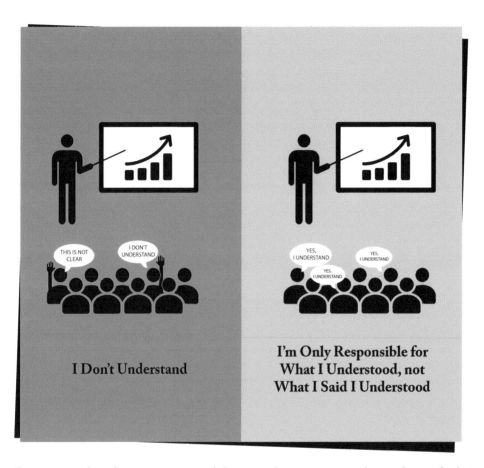

I Don't Understand

I'm Only Responsible for What I Understood, not What I Said I Understood

It is your pitch and it is your responsibility to make sure everyone has understood what you want them to understand. Honour in the Arab culture means that no one will tell you they do not understand. To get around this, keep an eye on their body language and judge it yourself, you might be talking too fast or using a very technical language. Repeat yourself, visit the same subject twice and change the words you use to easier ones. It might also be useful to use photos with a small description or short and easy to understand video.

In the Arab world, most children in the region learn English as a second language in school today, but it is mainly to read and write English, not to speak it. Younger generations will speak much better English than older generations (but in most of the cases the older ones are the decision-makers). It is important when you are presenting to be aware that you are speaking with people who may appear to understand you. However, since English is their second language, they may misunderstand much of what you think is clear. To avoid this, you need to always check carefully to ensure you are fully understood.

If you are dealing with a company outside the big cities, many more people may struggle to understand you. My advice is to have all of your material in both English and Arabic even if your meeting is in English. At the early stage of your meetings the people you meet will have to share what you present with others who might not speak English, so ensure everything you provide is translated, including subtitling any videos you present in Arabic.

Other changes you could make to enhance understanding include the use of short sentences with no complex structures. Also, use a more universal English and never try to ask them if they understand you in a direct and patronizing way, you will embarrass them. When you are misunderstood do not show frustration or any signs that you are annoyed. In all cases, you need to keep your speech and presentations "short and simple" and take your time so that you do not lose them with the detail and you are understood. Take a respectful approach and talk in a calm voice, and you will be surprised how far that goes.

Can You do Business Without Arabic?

In the Arab world, it is known that Western businesses often do not learn any Arabic before they arrive in the Arab countries, Many Westerners work for years in the Arab world without learning a single word of Arabic. Therefore, to break this stereotype will create respect. Arabs are aware that Arabic is not an easy language to learn and they do not expect you to speak it. However, learning a few words in Arabic and showing interest in its link to Islam will be highly appreciated by both the Muslims and Arab Christians. This remains important, even for those places where English is spoken often, such as Dubai.

Arabs do not expect you to speak to them in Arabic, but learning a few words before you meet with them is always helpful as they will appreciate that you are making an effort to learn even a small amount about their culture and language. Thousands of Westerners do business without any Arabic, and since most of the Arab business you will be dealing with have employees who have graduated from big Western universities and speak good English, it is most likely that the meeting and negotiations will be conducted in English. However, adjust your English-language competency to integrate Arabic into your business as much as possible. Only use Arabic if you know the words. As I mentioned before, Arabs are very proud of their language, so learning some words, such as greetings are always useful.

Also, it is very important to remember that if you can speak enough Arabic to understand a conversation, you should make everyone aware that you do so. Arabs will assume that you cannot speak or understand their language, so they might speak to each other in Arabic in your presence, perhaps discussing private matters because they assume you cannot understand. If they discovered that you speak Arabic later on, it will cause damage to the relationship and you could even be considered to be a Western spy.

Translations, is it Important?

Beside speaking some Arabic, to show that you are serious about working with them, you should always provide correctly translated material, presentations, videos and so on to your Arab counterparts. However, through my experience with Western companies targeting the Arab world in the West or in their countries, many business and brands do not realise that they cannot just directly translate material into Arabic, such as through translation programs. They often do not pay attention to use certain words, sentences and phrases which give a completely different meaning. It is advisable to have your material translated into Arabic by a native speaker. It will help you to have all promotional materials translated into Arabic, ensure this is printed before you leave your country as translation services in hotels are expensive and not great.

As you have learnt by now, you are targeting a very conservative market, therefore your documents and material designs and any imagery that you use should be chosen very carefully. Many people who translate to Arabic from English fall into technical errors which create unreadable Arabic. For instance, a business might take my advice and hire a native Arabic translator, but they then send the document to a non-Arab graphic designer assuming that everything is in order. However, after processing the translated Arabic text because Arabic letters are written all together, letters fall apart and words no longer make sense. The end result is a very beautiful design with disconnected words which no longer have any meaning. Unfortunately, I have seen this mistake in many documents that have been presented to Arab businesspeople or even put up as welcoming signs outside tourist attractions or shops in the West. If you or your graphic designers cannot read Arabic, your material will likely contain words and sentences presented in an unreadable way.

It is very important to have an Arabic speaker read through all your material before you send it to print. The wrong Arabic translation will send the wrong message to your counterpart and it might be interrupted that you are not so serious about doing business.

Business Cards

When in the Arab world, it is very important to have your business card with you even when your Arab partner might not have one, it is also advisable to have the information printed in English and Arabic; having one side in Arabic is always a nice touch, but not necessary. As mentioned previously, it is very important to have it translated correctly and to remember Arabic is read from right to left. Always exchange business cards (with the right hand) . Also, take a good look at their card and take note of the designations of the card, like HRH, Shaikh, or Doctor etc. and during the conversation make sure to refer to these titles. However, never ask a senior Arab person for their business card. If they ask for your card, it is a very good sign that they want to do business with you.

Continuity is Crucial

When your team travels back to the Arab world, if you can, ensure that the same team visits on every occasion. This is part of the personal relationship and trust that you must build, it will also help you to get on with the business as they do not have to waste time getting to know new people. Again, since Arabs relationships are based on trust, they will start to wonder why you are replacing people and what you are trying to hide.

Arabs love staying within their comfort zone, this is why continuity is very important when you work with them. Any change of key people can take you back to square one, people are the most important to them. Once you manage to build a business relationship it is important to maintain continuity. If a key member of your staff has developed a good relationship with their counterparts it is important to keep them visiting these people if not take them out quickly.

If for any reason, there is to be some personnel change make sure the person who is leaving makes the introductions to their replacement in person. This way, the Arabs will not feel that the relationship is ending and that the new contact is a continuity of the relationship that had developed previously. Arabs do not find new changes easy to adopt as this is part of their business security. If you spent years building your business with them and you want to disappear from the picture and send someone who cannot handle them correctly, you are risking going back to square one and she/he will have to start from scratch.

Never send anyone likely to be impatient, harsh, nervous, or unkind, this will not work well in the Arab world. You need a sensitive person, who gets on well with people and can adapt to different behaviours with a flexible approach. Age and maturity are also significant in the Arab world. Across the Arab world, a young and fresh graduate is not taken seriously in business or even in politics.

14 Negotiations

Bargain Like an Arab

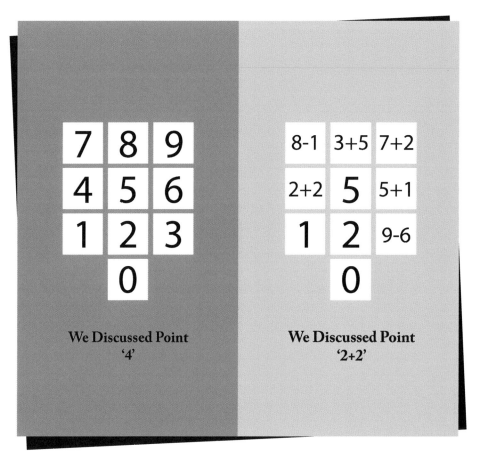

We Discussed Point '4'

We Discussed Point '2+2'

Negotiations with Your Arab Partners

It is very important to understand that Arabs are always in business and trade, it has been part of their culture and tradition for many different reasons, such as location. They have been engaged in trade for thousands of years. So, they are experienced in driving a hard bargain. Never approach them with the stereotypes that you can sell Arabs anything at any time with a quick and easy sale, and that the Arabs are rich and will buy anything; this is wrong and it shows that you did not do your homework.

Negotiations are not a simple one-day thing

In the West time is money. Imagine what it will be if they are negotiating money. In the Arab world time is something they can use in any way they want. Misunderstanding this can cause frustration. Delays, which are being considered in the West, will just be part of the negotiations in the Arab world. Everything will take time even if it is just a very basic standard thing. For you, you are there to sign a contract and go back home, but for the Arabs, it is just the start of a long-term relationship.

It will have become clear to you by now that Arabs do not rush anything. This includes negotiations, they will start with irrelevant small talks, introductions, and different conversational topics. Business and social conversation are combined. Before negotiations begin, you might not meet the decision-makers, however, during the negotiations, the decision-makers will be present, and this is when you need to be extra vigilant with what you are offering and presenting.

Never Try to Rush them

The chairman of a British construction company flew to Kuwait for a meeting with a high-level Kuwaiti official in the Ministry of Transport. The team in London and Kuwait had worked hard to secure the meeting and spent a month trying to get the initial approval for the proposal. The chairman had a very good meeting with the Kuwaiti senior official, however, he insisted that they must give him a definite answer while he was in the country. The Kuwaitis smiled and said "Inshaallah". That was the end of the negotiations, the proposal was never approved.

In negotiations, it is wise to not pressure your counterparts with deadlines as they might take offence. Do not think that because you agreed on everything in the previous meeting, they will be ready to sign. In the Arab world, the attitude towards negotiation and approval of contracts is completely different. Be prepared for additional meetings to take place and repetitions of the same points and conversations. Arabs also do not address topics directly, and they will not appreciate being put under pressure to make a decision on the spot. Once you have closed a deal with them, you will be the favourite for the next deal or contract. However, once you misinterpret their hospitality and politeness as a sign of a successful deal, you will risk making mistakes that may cause you to lose the deal.

A "yes" might mean, "I understand you", but not "yes, I agree." Therefore, during negotiations, you must place close attention to what they do not just what they say. If you apply pressure you may be told 'yes' when 'no' is meant. If your Arab colleague or counterpart is hesitant to answer a question directly, this could be a sign that they are hesitant to give you a direct 'no'. Many Westerners make the mistake of assuming that a positive response means that an agreement is finalised. But this will not be the case. For example, if they were to disagree, they might look at each other and reply "Inshallah". Look out for this and body language as indicators of a refusal.

To ensure that you do not cause them to say "yes" when they mean the opposite, you should give them options and time to get back to you. They will also dislike pressure and will not like you directly saying "no" to them.

Negotiations are unlikely to be quick, even if you have had many successful meetings beforehand. It would, therefore, be unwise to plan to leave the country straight after you conclude the deal. You may have to extend your stay to accommodate the long negotiation period. In doing so, you will be ensuring your counterparts that you are there and always prepared to spend time with them to ensure the business will be secured; this is profitable for both parties.

Negotiation can be much slower in the Arab world. You must be patient and prepared for negotiations to happen in their own time. They can last hours, days or even years. It all depends on what you negotiate, for instance, large projects could take three years or more. Negotiation length and approval is also influenced by the extent your business relationship is established.

Speak First

When negotiations begin, the Arabs will wait for you to present your offer first, no matter what you have discussed previously. They want to hear everything but be very careful and do not reveal everything you have to offer at once. Once you present, then the negotiations will begin. No matter what you offer at the start, your counterparts will always ask for more and they will bring to the table points and problems that you might not be aware of.

As such, negotiations with the Arabs can be tough. It might be a surprise to know that all their focus will be on the price, and they may only ask for a package on their terms. There is a large bargaining culture across the Arab world, irrespective of how rich they are. Prices are usually bargained for much less than displayed. This applies to business as well as the marketplace, at the shop or in the luxury offices of the city. During the summer when the Arabs are in the West for holiday, you will be surprised to know that the wealthy Arabs will go to Sunday street markets for the bargaining experience. This should give you an indication of how bargaining is part of their way of life; it is emotionally charged. In the West, business decisions are based on facts and figures, but Arabs mostly make decisions based on gut and heart feelings. They approach the negotiation as a competition, simply because they feel they need to protect their honour.

Behaviours During Negotiations

Be Prepared to Modify Your Original Ideas

In the Arab world, negotiations rarely follow a clear plan and can easily change structure and agenda. Therefore, you must be prepared to modify your plans. Go to the meeting knowing that you will need to argue and, most importantly, you will need to listen to all proposals irrelevant of their relevance. Of course, even your Arab counterparts will not expect you to agree to every proposal they put on the table, but all you need to do is think beyond what you offer. Do not try to put pressure on them to stick to an agenda as this will create problems. The Arabs will become emotional during the meeting, be careful to follow this and never lose your temper or show negative thoughts and feelings with your body language. Be polite but also be firm and repeat your position for the discussion to ensure everything is clear for their benefit and yours.

What to Give Away, "TANAZUL"

The Arabs go into negotiations with only one aim, to win. They will do anything to win! They do believe that someone must sacrifice something to achieve any progress and most of the time this person is you. In the Arab culture, there is something called "TANAZUL" which means to give away something that you do not want to give but you are forced to. "TANAZUL" also means that your opponent has a stronger position than you. When working with Arabs, it is the little things that count, such as small gestures. These will always work to your advantage. To increase the chance of succeeding in the negotiations, you should offer your counterpart something, such as a small discount.

Never give your best offer up front, or give too many concessions at an early stage, wait, and see what they have. Always give yourself a big margin on the price, if it is too low, they will ask for unexpected demands and the cost will rise. Also, be careful to never set a high price, they will find this dishonest. Be reasonable and know where you stand. They will discuss and negotiate your prices and agreements extensively and slowly, working towards the best offer. Build your offer in stages or layers to make them feel that you are the one giving

"TANAZUL". For them, it is all part of their game. If they are buying, they will offer you a very low price, so low it may be an insult to your product, and if they are selling their offer will be very high. It will be a frustrating process and their pressures will be intense.

The Arabs will try to take your package one by one and negotiate each item separately, do not allow it. In doing so, you will end up giving much more than what you are willing to offer. Ensure that you always have different options, and never make a final offer if it is not an option for you. They will ask for ridiculous demands, but you must not bluntly refuse them, open them for discussing knowing what you want. It might be one of their tactics to gain more from you; if you are not sure and have doubts, stop, and evaluate the risks again. If you know that what they are asking for is impossible, do not concede anything too easily. Take a break, the Arabs have five a day so take one yourself and say that you will need to discuss it with your head office and get back to them. Never show that you have lost interest or that you are not the decision-maker. Ensure that they understand that you are there to sign the deal and maintain the relationship, they will appreciate that and understand you need more time.

Once you are winning your negotiations do not show it as this will be considered rude. The senior persons in the room will take it as a personal insult, they will start looking for new points to negotiate and you will end up going back over the points that you have already agreed on.

Honour and Shame

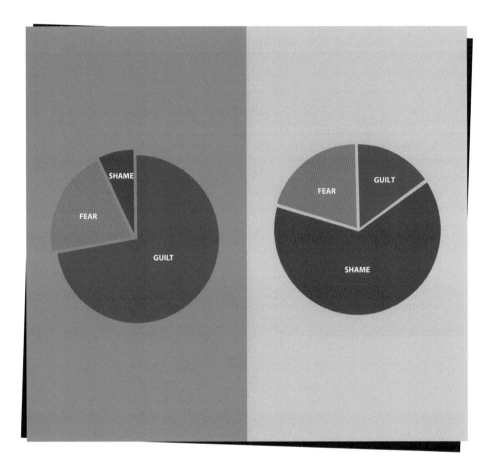

For Arabs, paying for the food bill or a cup of coffee at a restaurant is part of losing or gaining face in front of others and ensuring that a reputation of generosity is protected. Do not be surprised if you see two Arabs arguing and shouting about who will pay.

As you will know by now, in the Arab world reputation is everything, and it is impossible to disconnect from anything in life or business. The same goes for negotiation. One of the most important aspects of doing business or negotiation is to protect the reputation, theirs, and everyone else's. They can accept most things, but they cannot accept to 'lose face' in front of anyone.

In the Arab culture "Saving Face" is something you cannot ignore when you do business or negotiate with your Arabs counterparts. any sign of losing face, will result in negative meetings and negotiations. Remember that this is not personal, by making one lose face you might just make the whole group to lose face too.

Of course, for Westerners or non-Westerners it is hard to understand this and to avoid it sometimes. It could be a very simple act, such as saying no to someone, greeting someone before the leader of the group, rejecting a proposal without even looking at it or addressing someone with lower rank first before the boss.

In the West, if you make an error, the quickest way to get yourself out of trouble is to confess to your error as early as possible. People might see you as an honest person who has just made an error. On the other hand, for an Arab to admit the error is a problem, they will feel embarrassed and they will be lost. As a result, they would do everything possible to avoid responsibility and to minimize the damage. They will deny the obvious mistakes, even if they have to lie.

Face is a very important concept for the Arabs, it is your reputation and it reflects how people regard you. It is the same as 'making me look bad' in the west. However, face is much more important for the Arabs as they see it as a major focal point in any business and relationship. For Westerners, this comes second to business, which is always first; for the Arabs face makes the business. Therefore, saving face is important and must be taken seriously. However, it should not distract you from your normal way of doing business; if you must say something say it. Do not be somebody that you are not, be who you are, respectful, polite and professional, and ask the tough questions in business when you have to as the Arabs will do that to you.

Disagreement

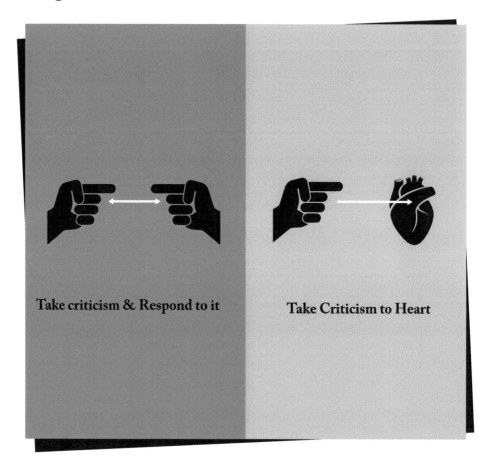

You must avoid any disagreement in the meeting, once you start to openly argue with an Arab, especially if other people are present, the deal is at risk. This can take any form of communication, such as raising your voice could damage your honour, which would be almost impossible to win back. You may want to point out a mistake that your counterpart has made, for instance. However, this will be the result of your counterpart thinking that his honour is at risk, it will be embarrassing. It is, therefore, best to avoid any constructive criticism.

To avoid this, you can respond by deflecting the negative. For example, if your counterpart said something irrelevant which has nothing to do with the business deal and might cause a delay, you could say "I think this is a great idea, however, I think it will be quicker if we do this and if you agree we might approach it this way". You could also deflect the blame onto yourself, by saying "I always make the same mistake and do not explain things clearly, please allow me to be clearer". If they begin to argue then something is wrong, never try to stop it. Wait until they finish and say something along the line of: "in the past, I had a similar situation and we did (1,2,3...) and it worked, may I suggest we try it this time?"

If you make him feel like he is in charge, he will agree with your point of view. In some cases, where you must address the point, do not do it in front of others. It is better to address an issue with the person alone; they will appreciate it. Telling someone you think she/he is wrong directly, will cause them to lose face and as a result, you may lose your contract.

On the other hand, you can use this to your advantage by winning people to your side during doing business or negotiation. By praising someone in front of others, such as for their hospitality, hard work or kindness, you will not just make him feel good, but it will also lift your status in front of his family or friends.

What you should take from this is that the way you argue or make your point is very important while negotiating with Arabs. You will benefit if you do not disagree, intimidate or lose anyone present. I am not saying that you should not disagree but do not make the disagreement personal, always question the subject not the person. Moreover, if you notice that they need help, you must never give them the impression that you are the Western saviour who is there to teach them how to do things. Showing respect, using cautious language and the right words for objections in a subtle way and without criticism is the right approach to maintain the relationship. This also applies to your counterparts, never allow others to make you lose face, they have to respect you at all times.

Dealing with Disputes: Sit Down and Talk

In the Arab world, only friendly discussions can resolve disputes. To resolve a problem, they like to sit down and talk. Once a voice is raised, or reference is made to the legalities of a contract in negotiations, then the personal touch and relationship will end. It is best to discuss the deal or contract without referencing anything legal. However, you must know your legal right beforehand and your position within the legal process. If a lawyer is brought into negotiations or you mention legalities, you will insult the relationship.

Business disputes are easier to deal with if you have a strong personal relationship. The use of networks and contact "Wasta" is used for everything, so why not use it in your negotiation and conflict resolution. Make sure you always have a back-up by lining up someone as an intermediary to help bring some pressure (it is important the pressure does not come from you). In the Arab world, the faster the conflict is resolved the less the damage it causes, so in cases of conflict always ask your "Wasta" to help re-start negotiation. Having your contact involved is the best chance to finish the matter.

Hierarchy

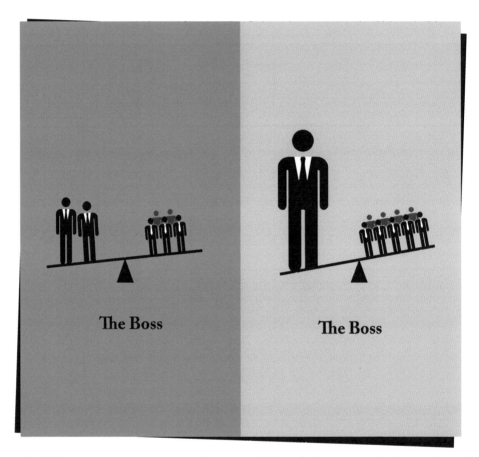

A British company representative in Egypt says: "I have built a very good relationship with a very nice Egyptian guy who works for the company we are dealing with, his English is perfect and almost all of our meetings were a great success and we agreed on almost everything. However, when we met with his boss, who does not speak good English and has no knowledge or mechanical experience, he changed everything we agreed on. I was waiting for my friend to intervene and tell him about what we have agreed on, but the Egyptian friend did not say a word.

In the Arab world, authority is part of the culture and is very well respected. Many people benefit from the family they are born in or from the connections they have. These will play a big part in their future success. They can reach high positions and, in many cases, this is not related to their experience.

Arabs always look to authorities to help them and tell them what to do. Almost all Arabs accept their 'place' in society; they are convinced that this is how life is supposed to be. As a result, they are hesitant to take decisions on their own. This also occurs in business; hierarchy is very important. The power and decisions are coming from the top; the leaders are separated from the group.

This hierarchical system means that, in Arab culture, decisions are in the hand of one person and, in some cases, a few people. These are the same people who create and tailor very tough rules to secure their power. In the Arab world, the boss doesn't see themselves as an employee of the company or the organisation, they have full control over all employees and staff are not empowered to discuss, question, object or say no to any decision made by the boss. They are there to do what they are told by the boss. They will not give any feedback and, most importantly for you, they are not the decision-maker. Their relationship with the boss is limited to non.

In meetings, the less senior member of the team will not contribute to the meeting. They will only sit and listen, and they will only talk if they are asked to do so by a more senior member. You must adopt the same attitude. If you are the boss, make sure that less senior members do not interrupt you in front of others.

In society and business and workplace, a superior individual must be respected by everyone below him. If you break this rule, you are putting those less senior in a very uncomfortable situation. This would upset the boss.

Who am I dealing with?

When doing business in the Arab world, at your early meetings mainly in the GCC countries, you will be meeting with an expatriate executive. In the GCC, the majority of the workforce are foreigners and migrants, either from India, Pakistan, Europe, or other Arab countries (Lebanon, Egypt, Jordan, Syria and Palestine) who speak Arabic and in many cases dress like the local gulf people. Most of those Arabs are in the GCC for long periods and are more committed to their host country than the Westerns who enjoy high earning rates over short periods of time.

However, when you are dealing with an ex-pat (in most cases the Non-Arabs ex-pats), it will most likely require a different approach. Do your homework in advance, know who you will be dealing with and who is the decision-maker. You may be dealing with a Western ex-pat and the meeting will then tend to follow your standard practice, but do not be misled, that is not what you want, the deal will be made with someone else.

It is common that senior business people in the Arab world, especially in the GCC countries, appear only at the negotiation stage. The team is there to do the detailed negotiations so that the senior businesspeople do not need to be involved with the paperwork and avoid any awkward or embarrassing confrontations during the early negotiations. If you work for a large corporate company, your most senior people should not be part of the early discussions and negotiations. In fact, the junior staff will struggle to know how to deal with them and they cannot ask their boss to be a part of the early negotiations. If you are a small company and you are the only one who can discuss such details, do not worry as they will understand and appreciate that. However, do not expect the senior decision-makers to be part of the early meetings.

The mistake many businesses do is to assume that these mediators have the power to make a decision. If after many meetings you still have not met with the decision-maker, you are wasting your time.

Decisions Makers

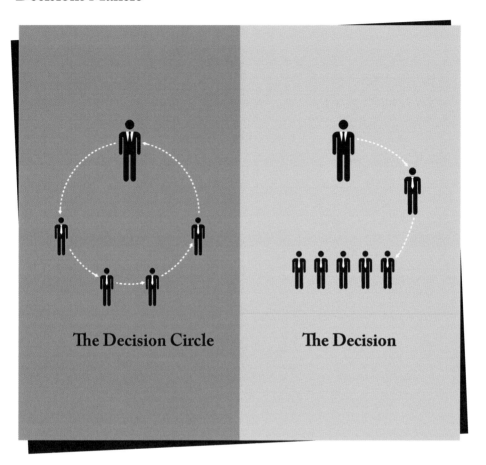

Knowing who is the decision-maker is a big challenge for many businesses in the region. Do not expect your client to tell you this information, you need to do your homework and use your "Wasta" personal connection in the decision-making processes and during the negotiation. Also, it is not just who is making the decision that you need to concentrate on but also, in many cases who is blocking the decision, particularly when there is a delay.

Once you know who the decision-makers are, you will know where to focus your power. When your counterpart is not the decision-maker, you will notice that the negotiation is going nowhere and you feel frustrated, simply because they cannot make the decision and will have to refer it to someone else.

However, once you meet the decision-makers, to your surprise the meetings may take a Western-style and they will be shorter than the previous meeting. Make sure that you use this opportunity and be prepared to present your point as that might be the only time that you meet with them. Never give all your offers until you meet the decision-maker, to show their authority they will ask for something from you.

Influential Personal Staff

Also, it is very important to remember that VIPs in the Arab world generally work through staff, those staff in some cases can be very influential, even when they are not the decision-makers. Let us start with the guy you meet at the airport or the one who meets you at the company reception, or the person who enters the meeting unexpectedly. They might be a relative, friend or a confidant of the person you are there to do business with.

Another thing that you should always pay attention to, if you are looking for a long relationship in the Arab world, is if senior people have their young sons and, in recent years, daughters part of the negotiation. Their presence may be as a training practice, so if you want to establish a long relationship, take him/her very seriously. If your business is successful, the son/daughter will be the one making the decisions in a few years.

Why do I Always have to go to them?

Arab business people always prefer to do business in their countries, especially for the first meetings. They feel more powerful when they are in their home countries, which makes them feel more comfortable during the decision-making process and in keeping the boss updated if needed. This does not mean that you cannot do business with them in your country, you will and they will come to you once the relationship is stronger, but the contract and final steps of the negotiations will always be in their country.

Body Language

Body Language Won't Affect the Business

Body Language can Make or Break the Deal

In 2005, the picture of the US President at the time George W. Bush holding hands with King Abdullah of Saudi in the gardens of his Texas ranch was a shock to too many Americans, but that was a sign of the American president showing respect and friendship. If you build a good relationship with the Arabs, they might take your hand when leading you somewhere. This, unusual from a Western viewpoint, is simply a cultural difference. Women are an exception to this rule. Never stand close to, stare at, or touch a woman and, if you are a woman, the same will apply to Arab men, try to avoid any close contact.

Body language is important no matter where you are in the world, but in the Arab world, it has greater importance. It could be damaging to your business, it can give a clear indication of a person's opinion more than their words. For example, when you nod in the West it means you agree, however, in the Arab world a nod does not mean "yes". It means: "I am listening" or "continue".

In negotiations, if it is hard to read and understand how your Arab counterparts think and behave, you should observe their body language, signs and reactions and all other non-verbal signs. This could include moments of silence (in these moments try not to sell and give them time to think). In the Arab world, it is common to be aggressive when talking or just arguing about a very simple thing; this is their way of showing passion. They are not angry.

Sometimes, when everything is going perfectly and you are speaking in English, suddenly your counterpart will look at her/his colleague and start talking in Arabic, and then leave the room without saying anything and return after a few minutes without any explanations. Do not be offended by this, he is not talking behind your back, he just wants to express himself in the right way using his language. Do not even show you have noticed their behaviour. Observe and listen carefully, pay attention to any comments on your presentation. They will do these things more often when they feel they have built a trustful relationship with you, but you can expect this kind of behaviour from the first meeting. If the body language conflicts with the spoken word, then believe the body language.

You also need to pay attention to your body language. Arab people pay attention to your confidence level from the very first handshake. They look at how you walk into the room, how you carry yourself, what you are wearing, and if you make eye contact. Any signs that they find offensive might cost you the contract that you are there for. So do not show any signs that you are not comfortable or having a bad time.

It is therefore not always what you say, but what you do that is important. Pay attention to how you place yourself and how to sit in your chair. Ensure that you sit upright in your chair and leaning back, and relaxing can be seen unprofessional. Also, do not put your hand in your pocket or sit in certain positions, do not show them that you are having a bad day, they will take it personally.

Look them in the Eye!

Eye contact is made when you do business and negotiate in the Arab world. It is important that you do this, if you are not confident enough to look people in the eye when you talk to them, the Arabs will think that you are up to something and they will think you are not telling the truth.

The insult of the Foot

One of the mistakes most Westerners do when they meet with Arabs is placing their feet in the wrong way. For the Arabs, their feet are always on the floor. Crossing your legs can be taken as an insult. The most insulting thing a Westerner can do is to show an Arab the sole of their shoe when they sit. Also, placing your feet on a table, even if you are at your home or a hotel, it is unacceptable and can be taken as an insult to those present.

Personal Space

Personal space in the Arab world does not exist between people of the same sex. You will experience much less personal space than you are used to in the West, as they will stand and sit very close to you. Arabs like to stand too close, do not show that you are not comfortable with it, do not move backwards; it is respectful to show them that the way they behave is not rude.

Closing the Deal:

You are not the Only Player

Arab business will always make you know that they are talking to other companies and they are in an advanced stage of negotiation with them. Sometimes, if they are keen to work with you and want a better deal from you, they will talk to your competitors in your country or other countries and make sure you know about it. Do not be surprised if both you and your competitors have a meeting scheduled for the same deal on the same day or week. This could be true but also it could be another tactic that an Arab negotiator could play to bargain a better deal. When they start to list the offers your competitors are offering, you can play the same game. Even if you are talking to others outside their country, tell them they are the only company you are talking to at the moment, they might take it as a gesture from you that you are there to build a trustful relationship. In some cases, they might use it to apply pressure tactics in the negotiation.

Always remember that, in the Arab world, they will use everything to tempt you to do what they want. You will be told if you do something and give them more concessions and do what they want you, then more likely to get the deal, not to the other company that they are talking to. Approach this with caution, never promise what you do not have and cannot deliver.

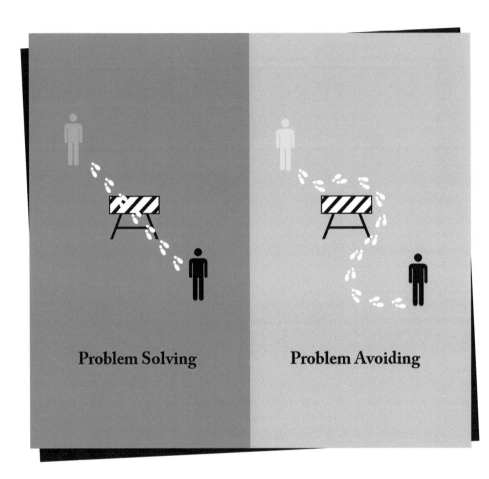

Problem Solving   **Problem Avoiding**

One of the main annoying cultural differences for Westerners when negotiating with the Arabs is that they keep returning to items that you have already discussed and dealt with. Often, they will keep going back and forward in circles and will not tell you their concessions until almost everything has been discussed. This is a tactic they use to renegotiate. You have already discussed this, so hold your ground.

If you reach this stage, you are doing very well, however, things might not go very smoothly so be careful to always show positivity. It is wise to be prepared for this back and forward stage and have something to give away that was not offered previously.

If You Have to Walk Away from the Deal…Do it

Arabs will press a very hard bargain. Set your limit beforehand and be ready to walk away from the deal, no matter how small or big your company is. Once you reach your end of bargaining and what you can offer, stop, be firm with your offer and at the same time be polite.

Exchanging Favours: Building Relationships

I once talked to a Saudi friend who told me that he was very disappointed in a mutual English friend and asked me not to invite him to join us for dinner. When I asked him for the reason, he explained that the English friend, while living in Saudi, had gratefully accepted many favours while he was getting settled in the country. The Saudi friend had helped him with everything he needed including supplies, furniture and finding a maid. When the Saudi asked him to help him with his daughter's study in the UK, the English friend told him that he did not want to get involved with these things and unfortunately, he cannot help. The Saudi took this as a personal insult and felt hostile that the English friend did not care enough about him to help him. He said that he could have told him that he will see and try and that would have been more than enough for me.

Do not be surprised if, during negotiations, you are asked for provisions that seem self-interested. The exchange of favours is an important part of building relationships in business. Be prepared to carry out personal favours during your negotiations in the Arab world. In Arab culture, it is normal to accept and return favours. If they ask you for a favour and you can do it, you should, it will work to your advantage. Never just say no or you cannot do it, or you are not obliged to do it. If you cannot do it just say you will try, it will be understood, and it will be appreciated that you tried to help. Your efforts will be highly appreciated and well-remembered.

In Arab culture, it is noble not to openly refuse a request from a friend. This does not mean that the favour must be done, but it is a way of responding to avoid saying no.

Contracts

In the Arab world, words are very powerful. Arabs prefer verbal agreements first, and if you cannot deliver what they are asking for, do not promise to deliver it. If you start talking about the contract with your Arab counterparts it could mean the relationship is not properly established. This could be true in some cases, however, contracts are very important, even if in some part of the Arab world say it as an agreement rather than an obligation. What is written down in a contract might still be open to negotiation should the circumstances change.

The Enforcement of Contracts

Contracts are not straightforward in the Arab world; the process is long and the bureaucracy and number of people who must sign it are even longer. It is also a long process to find out who is responsible for causing the delays or the problems to contract signage. You can celebrate only when you have the signed and legalised the document. Of course, words are so powerful for the Arabs and they respect it. Follow my advice and start with the verbal agreements just to show them that you want to do business. Then ensure that everything must be in writing.

In some cases, you might sign a contract, but nothing happens after that and no business takes place. I have seen many big decisions being reversed and changed and the termination of contracts early.

Once you are at a contract stage, make sure everything is clear to both sides, you are there to do business, not to end up in a legal dispute. Ensure that your counterparts understand every small detail of the contract to avoid any misunderstandings. Always take your time to read the wording of the documents and your contracts very carefully, misinterpretation is common and if they have drafted the contract they might use words that are in their advantage and open the door for more concessions from you in the future. The Arabs are known for asking for changes in contracts after they have signed them, they might want to add a new fee or increase the price or to use a certain third party, which is not the best or the cheapest option for you. For them, they believe this is normal practice, so do not be shocked. They might want to change the contract in order to stick to it. It is also good to know that, when it is to their advantage, the Arabs will follow a Western approach and insist that you must follow the contracts.

Ready-Made Contracts

In the Arab world, they have some ready-made contracts and, in some cases, they might suggest that you just use it, as it is easier for both of you. They might give you the impression that it is the only contract they have, and you have no other options. Remember that you do not have to accept this, it will be in their favour, not yours, and many of the points that you fought for during the negotiations will not be included. Stand firm and stick to your position, it is only you who can insist that you will not use that model of contract.

Contract Language

Contracts are usually written in English, or in some cases in both English and Arabic. However, if the contract is drafted in English, it will have to be translated into Arabic. In all cases and particularly in the event of a conflict, the Arabic version will be enforced, that is why you must not ignore the importance of the translations especially in the final agreement!

Three Years since we Signed the Contract, they are Asking for Changes Now!

For the Arabs, a signed contract means that they are interested to do work together. Do not be surprised if, after years of a smooth relationship and several years after you signed the contract, that circumstances with your Arab partners changed and they start to ignore the contract. They might also ask for new conditions or even for a new contract.

TRUST ME,
I'M
عربي

The Risks and Opportunities

Proceed with Caution

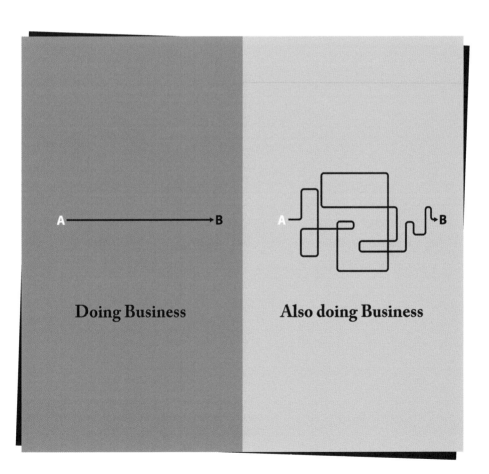

Doing Business

Also doing Business

Doing business in the Arab world is rewarding but it can also be challenging. It continues to attract businesses, brands, and investors, who are trying to access one of the world's youngest and growing markets which offers great opportunities. Of course, this comes with the risks, especially when doing business in a new market which comes with many political, financial, and cultural obstacles. The threat of violence and the unrest all over the Arab world and the massive instability of the oil prices, since the 2017 tension between some of the GCC countries, has made it difficult for Western companies to do business with a market that they have always believed is easy to do business with.

Doing business or working in the Arab world also comes with other problems, such as corruption, payment delays, currency changes and security in some parts of the region. Companies have to deal with changing of rules and regulations, bureaucratic systems, a lack of transparency, and some back-door dealings including preferential treatment of governments owned business. To add to that, each country of the Arab world will have different challenges and regulations, therefore it is very important to know the market you are entering and not to assess the Arab world as one risk. Consider all these barriers when deciding whether to and how to do business in the Arab world.

Despite all the difficulties in the Arab market, the opportunities are huge, and companies can increase profits as well as incur other great benefits from working and doing business in the Arab world. Even though you have to follow the regulations and principles to better mitigate their risks, you are opening your business to valuable prospects and which you can use to your benefit. The Arab world is always chasing foreign investment and will provide financial encouragement and benefits in return for companies wanting to locate there. There is a lot of business in the region, it is a growing market with a young population and increasingly diverse economies.

Delayed Payments from the Government

In recent years one of the main difficulties when doing business in the Arab world is financial, especially when you have a business or a contract with a government body. The unrest in the region and the decline of oil prices does affect the economy for many reasons. Moreover, receiving payment from government institutions is a slow process, so be sure to plan for that.

Many governments in the Arab world have had to cut costs which will make some economies undergo problems and contracts can change halfway through. This will affect when you receive your payments; sometimes this delay is for projects you already completed. One option you can consider is to enforce it in the contract that payments are made on time; however, this does not always work, and it is not always the best option to do. Some

174

companies who have a signed contract with government bodies have had to wait for years for their payment.

Corruption

Corruption exists in every business, trade and country in the world and the Arab world is not an exemption. In some Arab countries, you will have to face corrupt individuals which is one of the big risks of doing business in the Arab world. It is not unusual for contracts in some parts of the Arab world to include "commissions" or some kind of extra charges, charges that mean others you can name whatever price you like; these are bribes. However, you have to be very careful when doing this in both the public and private sectors. Involvement with bribery is a very serious crime in the Arab world and you could be risking yours and your business's reputations. To add to that, the penalties can include very severe punishments. Some governments, companies and individuals do not approve of bribery and see it as a very bad thing damaging their economies. Recently, the anti-bribery act has been taken seriously in almost all Arab countries, but that does not mean bribery has disappeared.

Intellectual Property Rights

Intellectual property rights is an area that has been notoriously difficult in the Arab world. Unfortunately, there is no enforcement of this in many parts of the Arab world. Many business and owners have made complaints about intellectual property rights in a different part of the Arab world. Although recent reports suggest good improvements in this area.

Scam Businesses

Scam businesses exist all over the world, including the Arab world. Many Western companies and businesses have related incidents of receiving fake business proposals from scammers who claimed to be Arab companies, requesting procurement charges amongst other false charges of extortionate amounts. This occurs because these scammers are well aware of the great opportunities available between the Arab regions and the West and take advantage of the fact that business is willing to ignore some checks to receive the great opportunities. To avoid this, always make sure that the people you are dealing with are legitimate, even if they are based in the region and have offices there.

Bureaucracy

Many foreign business struggle with laws and regulations in the Arab world. At some stage of doing business with the Arab world, you will have to come across this. Bureaucracy is number one concern when expanding into the Arab world, a tiring procedure and defective conduct is in every part. Especially when you start the process of obtaining the required licenses and permits. It is important that you get used to the bureaucracy or you will suffer. It is different from what you know in the West.

Administration

Administration, licensing, product approvals and many more laborious operating task can leave managerial desks flooded in paperwork. For many firms, overcoming the bureaucratic hassle is the biggest task to successfully breaking the Chinese market.

What to do with the Risks

The economic and business situations change all the time in different parts of the Arab world, you have to be aware of these changes at all times. Do the work yourself, it is your money and your business, do not take the glossy and well-designed market reports which you get from different analysts or organisations telling you that everything is great and it's the right time to do business in a particular Arab country. Many of these analysts have their own agendas, benefits and contact with different governments and private sectors in the Arab world, do not take all their information as trustworthy. Do your homework.

TRUST ME,
I'M
عربي

16 Conclusion

You have now reached the final chapter and have finished reading my book, thank you. However, you must be asking yourself many questions. If you were thinking of doing business with the Arab world you might wonder, where do you should begin.

By reading the book, I aim to help you reduce the stress in working with the Arabs, however, 2020 already is stressful enough for many businesses all over the world. By taking all my advice and the knowledge you have gained from the book, you will be more prepared for whatever happens when you deal with the Arabs – and I am sure that you know by now that success will begin when you start dealing with them.

To begin, I suggest that you start by evaluating the opportunities the Arab world has to offer and measure how far you and your business are in the journey toward becoming fully prepared to enter the Arab market.

The most definite stress in the Arab world before you close a deal is where to start. To move your business to a new country, you will be taking care of a lot of preparations and studying the market. You are responsible for the success of your business. Once you manage to start correctly and find your way in the Arab world, then closing the deal will be much easier.

The Arab world offers numerous opportunities for confident businessmen and women who are willing to go the extra mile and reach out to Arabs to harvest the great rewards the region has to offer. These opportunities will only offer themselves to those who consider the Arab world business culture and etiquette. Working with Arabs is the only starting point for those wishing to know what to expect when launching into the region and understanding the Arab culture will help you know how to start the business but not how to win it.

As we have learnt, there are different Arab business individualities that Westerners should know. Companies must realise that their staff knowledge or lack of knowledge will mean business success, no business success, or even damage to an existing and established business. Therefore, when companies hire and recruit new staff that have had previous overseas experience, they must have an understanding that cultures are different and what works for a market in Africa or China might not work for the Arab world. Despite the previous overseas experience, these people will still be required to know the new market they are going to.

You are now in a position to take the Arab culture into account and start to think about conducting successful business in the Arab world. by adopting the two key questions: what is the problem and what is the solution? And by stop complaining about Arab business practice as much as to understand it correctly.

You will be more successful when you ask yourself: how do I show the Arabs that I am open for business; how do I put all the stereotypes aside?; what are the issues?; how do I win their trust?; how do I build the relationship and win their friendship?; how do I sell my services to them and bring their investments to my country? All the answers depend on the balance between how much are you willing to build a relationship with the Arabs, and what do you have to offer to them.

You should not take the advice in this book as the only underlying reasons for your success. Success or failure will be based on your business principles, what you have to offer and how far you can convince your Arab counterparts that you or your company are the right partners for them to do business with. GOOD LUCK.

TRUST ME,
I'M

عربي

Q&A

Test your knowledge of the Arab world!

1. **The three continents border the Arab World?**
   a. Asia
   b. Africa
   c. North America
   d. Europe

2. **Which one of these Hollywood blockbusters have been filmed in the Arab world?**
   a. Stars Wars films
   b. Gladiator
   c. The Indiana Jones Trilogy
   d. The English Patient

3. **How many Arab countries are there in the world?**
   a. 15
   b. 40
   c. 25
   d. 22

4. **Which city is sacred to three monotheistic religions?**
   a. Rome
   b. Mecca
   c. Jerusalem
   d. Cairo

5. About how many Arabic words are used in Spanish?
a. 100
b. 700
c. 1,000
d. 7,000

6. How many letters are there in the Arabic alphabet?
a. 31
b. 45
c. 17
d. 28

7. The Arab World almost (….) the size of Europe.
a. 1/2
b. 1.5 x
c. 2 x
d. 3x

8. Which of these countries was the first country to recognise the United States
a. UK
b. Morocco
c. China
d. Germany

9. Which of these countries gave women the vote first?
a. Switzerland
b. Tunisia
c. Ecuador
d. Portugal

10. Bedouins (nomadic people) make up about (…) percent of Arab people
a. 5%
b. 10%
c. 25%
d. 2%

11. Ibn Khaldun was the founder of:
a. Sociology
b. Pharmacology
c. Economics
d. Mythology

12.   Which country in the world has most Muslims?

a. Iran

b. Egypt

c. Indonesia

d. Saudi Arabia

13.   Which celebrity is of Arab descent?

a. Steve Jobs

b. Shakira

c. Salma Hayek

d. Rami Malek

14.   You are negotiating with an Arab business - their starting price is very high. What should you do?

a. Accept it - the price is final

b. End the negotiations

c. Haggle until you reach the price you want

15.   Which of the following is NOT among the Five Pillars of Islam?

a. Fasting

b. Pilgrimage

c. Prayer

d. Following Islamic law (sharia)

16.   Which of these terms involves more countries?

a. Muslim

b. The Arab World

c. Middle East

d. MENA

17.   The term "Middle East" involves

a. Arab countries

b. Non-Arab countries

c. Arab and Non-Arab

18.   When greeting a Muslim woman which of these should you do?

a. Wait for her to extend a hand before shaking hands

b. Shake hands to avoid the possibility of causing offense

c. Not greet her as this will cause her to lose face

d. Do not shake her hand even if she extends it

19. **Which of these is not an Arab country?**
a. Iran
b. Iraq
c. Jordan
d. Saudi Arabia

20. **Which of these Arab countries is located in the Middle East?**
a. Lebanon
b. Mauritania
c. Sudan
d. Qatar

21. **Which of these Arab countries is located in North Africa?**
a. Algeria
b. Bahrain
c. Palestine
d. Yemen

22. **Which of these Arab countries is located in Africa?**
a. Somalia
b. Djibouti
c. Oman
d. Syria

23. **What language is used for business in Morocco?**
a. Arabic
b. English
c. French
d. Berber

24. **How many Arab countries are there in Asia?**
a. 15
b. 20
c. 13
d. 12

25. **In which of the following Arab countries has the United States conducted armed interventions?**

a. Algeria

b. Iraq

c. Libya

d. Somalia

e. Syria

f. Yemen

26. **Which of the following words best describes the Islam attitude towards business?**

a. Indifferent

b. Encourages

c. Forbids

d. Discourages

27. **Animals are routinely sacrificed on Eid Adha in memory of the sacrifice of Prophet Adam?**

a. Jesus (ISSA)

b. Prophet Abraham

c. Prophet Muhammad

28. **An Arab market place is called?**

a. Hajj

b. Souq

c. Makan

d. Qasar

29. **If you are having dinner with a business partner in the Arab world, when is it appropriate to talk business?**

a. As soon as you sit down at the table

b. After some polite table conversation

c. After the meal is through follow your business partner's cues, and pick up the business discussion when she or he steers in that direction.

30. **In the Arab world, you have been invited to a meal at a family home. You are very full. Your hostess offers you more food. What should you do?**

a. Politely refuse

b. Accept and eat everything on your plate

c. Accept and take a small bite

d. Accept and ask if you can take it with you

31.   **Constructive criticism can be taken as an insult.**
True
False

32.   **If offered a refreshment you should accept it.**
True
False

33.   **Always use your right hand for drinking and eating.**
True
False

34.   **Only women should have to dress modestly**
True
False

35.   **It's Okay to eat and drink in front of people when they are fasting in Ramadan?**
True
False

36.   **Most people in the Arab world are Muslim.**
True
False

37.   **Muslim and Arab mean the same thing.**
True
False

38.   **Just like the letters, the numbers in the Arabic language are written from right to left?**
True
False

39.   **The Arab world played no role in the development of world civilisation in ancient or modern times.**
True
False

40.   Religion does play a role in Arab business in many different ways

True

False

41.   Friends play no role in Arab culture

True

False

42.   Most Arabs don't share the westerns concept of "personal space" in public, and in private meetings or conversations. It is considered rude to step or lean away (unless you're a woman)

True

False

43.   When in the Arab world, try to engage in discussions on political issues (national and international), religion, alcohol

True

False

Answers

1 → a, b, d
2 → a, b, c, d
3 → d
4 → c
5 → d
6 → d
7 → c
8 → b
9 → b
10 → d
11 → a
12 → c
13 → a, b, c, d
14 → c

15 → d
16 → a
17 → c
18 → a
19 → a
20 → a, d
21 → a
22 → a, b
23 → c
24 → 12
25 → a, b, c, d, e, f
26 → b
27 → c
28 → b

29 → d
30 → c
31 → True
32 → True
33 → True
34 → False
35 → False
36 → True
37 → False
38 → True
39 → False
40 → True
41 → False
42 → True
43 → False

Useful Phrases

English	Arabic
• Hello	• Marhaba
• Good morning	• Sabah al-khayr
• Good evening/afternoon	• Masa al-khayr
• Thank you	• Shukran
• How are you?	• Kaif Haluk
• Congratulations	• Mabrook
• Welcome	• Ahlan Wa Sahlan
• Goodbye	• Ma' assalaama
• Go ahead	• Tafadul
• Pleased to meet you	• Tasharafna
• I don't understand	• La Afham
• I'm sorry	• Ana Aasif
• Goodbye	• Ma'a Alsalamah
• Please repeat	• Mara thaaniya, min faDlik?
• No	• Laa

- I
- He
- She
- We
- You (M/F)
- Do you speak English?
- I do not speak Arabic
- Finished
- No problem
- Congratulations

- Anaa
- Huwa
- Hiya
- NaHnu
- Anta/Anti
- Hal tatakallam Al-injliiziya?
- Laa atakallam Al-'arabiya
- Khallas
- Maafi Mushki
- Mabrook

References

- Aljazeera (2017) 'What is the GCC?', Aljazeera, [online]. 4th December 2017. Available from: https://www.aljazeera.com/news/2017/12/04/what-is-the-gcc/ [Accessed 1 February 2020].

- Ansari, Z And Nawwab, I. (2016) 'The Different Aspects Of Islamic Culture, UNESCO Publishing.

- Arab Barometer (2019) 'More Than Half of Young Arabs Want to Emigrate'. [online]. June 24th 2019. Available from: https://www.arabbarometer.org/media-news/more-than-half-of-young-arabs-want-to-emigrate/ [Accessed 1 June 2020].

- Asda'a Bcw (2019), 'A Call for Reform: A White Paper on the findings of the 11th annual ASDA'A BCW Arab Youth Survey'.

- BBC 'How did oil come to run our world?', BBC, [online]. Available from: https://www.bbc.co.uk/teach/how-did-oil-come-to-run-our-world/zn6gnrd [Accessed 13 January 2020]

- BBC 'The Arab world in seven charts: Are Arabs turning their backs on religion?, BBC, [online]. Available from: https://www.bbc.co.uk/news/world-middle-east-48703377 [Accessed 20 January 2020]

- BBC 'The Islamic world in the Middle Ages', BBC, [online]. Available from: https://www.bbc.co.uk/bitesize/guides/zx9xsbk/revision/7 [Accessed 20 April 2020]

- BBC (2017) "Profile: Arab League', BBC, [online]. 24th August 2017. Available from: https://www.bbc.co.uk/news/world-middle-east-15747941 [Accessed 15 February 2020]

- BBC (2017) "Profile: Arab League', BBC, [online]. 24th August 2017. Available from: https://www.bbc.co.uk/news/world-middle-east-15747941 [Accessed 15 February 2020]

- Bochner, S. (1982) Cultures in contact: Studies in cross-cultural interaction, Oxford: Pergamon Press.

- British Council (November 2017) 'Languages for the future' London

- Connelly, A, (1978) The Sykes-Picot Agreement and Its Consequences for Lawrence of Arabia, Queens College, Department of History.

- Danforth, N (2016) 'How the Middle East was invented', The Washington Post, USA.

- Esposito, J. (2011) 'What Everyone Needs to Know about Islam" Oxford University Press

- Grau. C (2018) Backpacking My Style, Amber Horn, an imprint of BHC Press

- Hamid, T, (2019) 'The state of social media in the Middle East', Wamda, Dubai, UAE

- Marco, M, (2019) The Wounds of Life, Page Publishing, New York May 19

- Metz, H. C. (1992) Saudi Arabia: A Country Study, Washington: GPO for the Library of Congress.

- Mirkin, B (2010) 'Population Levels, Trends and Policies in the Arab Region: Challenges and Opportunities', UNDP Report, New York

- Samovar, L. A. and Porter, R. E. (1994) International Communication: A Reader, Wad sworth Publishing Company.

- UNICEF, (2019),' MENA Generation 2030 Investing in children and youth to day to secure a prosperous region tomorrow
- United Nation (2020) 'The Impact of COVID-19 on the Arab Region an Opportunity to Build Back Better', New York

- World Bank (2019) 'Population, female - Middle East & North Africa'

- World Bank, [online]. Available from: https://data.worldbank.org/indicator/SP.POP.TOTL.FE.IN?locations=ZQ

Printed in Great Britain
by Amazon